The King

the Adulteress

The King

the Adulteress

A Psychoanalytic and Literary Reinterpretation

of *Madame Bovary* and *King Lear*

by Roberto Speziale-Bagliacca

FOREWORD BY FRANK KERMODE

ENGLISH VERSION EDITED BY COLIN RICE

Duke University Press Durham and London

1998

AGF-7081

Contents

Foreword

FRANK KERMODE

At first Roberto Speziale-Bagliacca's *Crescere Corvi* (the Italian title of this volume) was merely one of those books which arrive on one's desk fortuitously and in daunting numbers at someone else's whim. Yet another book about Shakespeare—it isn't a thought to make one tremble with excitement. But this one, I noticed, combined a study of *King Lear* with an essay on *Madame Bovary*, which is at least an unusual combination; moreover, it was written in Italian, and not by a professor of English. So there was a certain stirring of curiosity. The title did not tell me much, but I discovered from the author's preface that it derived from a Spanish proverb, "Cría cuervos y te sacaran los ojos," rear crows and they'll peck out your eyes. This suggested a gloomy attitude to family life, but I knew the author was a psychoanalyst of distinction, and imagined that professional experience led him to endorse this sinister proverb. His subtitle was "Psychoanalyses of *Madame Bovary* and *King Lear*," two masterpieces that on the face of it have nothing in common except disastrous family relationships (unless it is relevant that Flaubert greatly admired Shakespeare's play, which he read while at work on *Madame Bovary*). At any rate an analyst might be expected to produce some interesting variations on the layman's view of these works.

And so it proved. Speziale-Bagliacca has what might seem to ordinary readers and even to academic interpreters a quite extraordinary temerity, though he probably regards his style of commentary as merely a literary extension of his everyday business, which is to help his patients toward entirely new and probably very surprising versions of their personal history, to break through the prejudices and assumptions and disastrous self-interpretations that are spoiling their lives.

Most of us are willing to accept in some form the idea that the greatness of a work of art is related to the possibilities it offers of a vast, some would say virtually infinite, variety of interpretations; but most of us, however inconsistently, also reserve the right to claim that some interpretations may be wrong. Even Umberto Eco, champion of *opera aperta,* the "open work," concedes that interpretation has its limits and even thinks of overinterpretation as a sort of textual cancer.[1] Those of us who are or have been teachers have often and magisterially declared a reading to be incorrect, assuming our institutional authority over our students and no doubt wishing them to become as much like ourselves as possible. Most students comply; only a very few in this family are *corvi.* But Speziale-Bagliacca is not a member of the family, and he can look at its foundation texts as an anthropologist might examine an alien society, or an ethologist the behavior of crows.

Speziale-Bagliacca's own position seems to be that the works of literature most readers are content to think of as having peculiarly impressive qualities—as deserving to be called "great" or "canonical"—are "overdetermined," which allows the possibility that many quite unexpected things can be legitimately said about them. Because of a passing remark made by Flaubert, everybody knows he claimed to be Madame Bovary, but it can be argued that it would be at least as true to say that he was Charles Bovary; which is what Speziale-Bagliacca argues, along with much else. This may have the effect of making Bovary, the stupid physician and bungling surgeon, rather more interesting and rather more effective than he is usually taken to be. He has been maligned, described as the sort of man who "makes do with leftovers," a *mari complaisant;* now he emerges as a deceptive and dangerous sadomasochist, one of those who, in the formula of Theodor Reik, achieve "victory though defeat." With largely unconscious craft he arranges his own torment and plots Emma's descent into adultery and suicide, much as Flaubert himself did, though with more conscious art.

Speziale-Bagliacca's analytical insights into the life and work of Flaubert give a new connotation to the term "bovarysme." Can he be expected to achieve anything comparable when he turns to *King Lear?* Here his arguments will probably seem more outrageous, partly because even critics as skeptical as Tolstoy have never ventured to say that conventional opinion, accepting traditional stereotypes, has entirely misunderstood the moral bearings of the play. How are we to accept the view that Cordelia is a schemer, noble, stoical, loyal Kent a fraud, Oswald a decent sort of fellow? Partly it depends on our acceptance of a less aggressive argument: that Lear has, as a man, a desperate, childish need for love that he cannot, as a king, acknowledge. The responses of his daughters, when he tries to win their love without surrendering his royal dignity, are crucial to Speziale-Bagliacca's thesis. The character of Cordelia, as we know, looks somewhat different in the Quarto and Folio versions of the play, since a scene intended to represent her as a figure of redemptive holiness is missing from the Folio. But even if we stretch our imaginations to accommodate these two slightly different profiles of Cordelia, we are unlikely, until now, to have perceived her as a schemer. The Fool also turns out to be a sinister figure.

We may want to ask why Speziale-Bagliacca urgently wants to invert the standard readings of the play, which take Edmund to be a bad man, Edgar a good one, the elder sisters wicked, as in the Cinderella story. One explanation is that here, as in the study of *Madame Bovary,* he seeks to destroy venerable stereotypes, to exploit the possibilities of plural interpretation and of the necessarily overdetermined. What for this author is his daily business (the detection of concealed motives, the discovery of true stories under facades of falsity) is for the lay reader unusual and surprising. But the experience of having one's own conventional responses undermined must—however strongly one may continue to resist the new account of the matter—be beneficial, even if, like some other medicines, it may be hard to take.

Preface

I was prompted to write both of these essays by deeply emotional reactions. The idea for the first, "Charbovari," originally came to me when I happened to hear a radio dramatization of *Madame Bovary* in which the part of Charles was read by Glauco Mauri. The Italian actor's voice had such an ambiguous quality that I sensed the possibility of a special, though not immediately specific, interpretative key. My rereading of *King Lear,* on the other hand, originated, even before I was able to analyze my thoughts, in my *opposition* to Giorgio Strehler's interpretation of the play, in a production that went on to become legendary—in Europe at least. Several years have gone by and I have since made my peace with Strehler (indeed I am even grateful to him for his provocation). In the meantime, I have gradually been working out those initial, deeply instinctive reactions, that process which Gadamer would call *Wirkung.*

To Mario Vargas Llosa, who dedicated *La Orgia perpetua* to Flaubert and *Madame Bovary,* I owe the silken thread that links the two essays. Shakespeare was one of the writers Gustave Flaubert read while he was preparing the first draft of *Madame Bovary.* As a matter of fact, the letter to Louise Colet dated 30 March 1854 was written just after he had read *King Lear* and contains a comment describing the effect of Shakespeare on Flaubert: "All of his works produce the same sense of astonishment and exaltation in me as I feel when I think of the star system. I see only an immensity that dazzles my sight [L'ensemble de ses oeuvres me fait un effet de stupéfaction et d'exaltation comme l'idée du système sidéral. Je n'y vois qu'une immensité où mon regard se perd avec des éblouissements]."[1]

While the essay on Charles Bovary (and partly, of course, on Emma) did not create the problem of having to resort openly to psychoanalysis to any great extent, the same cannot be said about the essay on *Lear*, which necessitated more thoroughgoing digressions—as has been the experience of other analysts when writing about Shakespeare. At times I have relegated my explanations to the notes, so that the reader may decide for himself when to read them (or whether to read them at all). I would like to remind the reader that psychoanalysis proceeds inward, from the detail that exists on the outer edge toward the center, and from the center outward, back toward the edge. I have chosen to start almost always from the edge, even at the risk of occasionally disconcerting the reader who may not be familiar with this method of investigation.

I personally agree with those who think that literary criticism can benefit from an interdisciplinary approach. At the same time, I believe that the application of methods belonging to other branches of science could lead to confusion and create burdens that might hamper the freedom of the purely literary critic. Interdisciplinarity should therefore be seen not as an ontological necessity but as a methodological opportunity that might move us toward achieving true eclecticism (in the original sense of the term), provided we avoid the dangers of syncretism.

Ricoeur was probably right in saying that Nietzsche, Freud, and Marx have led to the modern rediscovery of the demonic side of Hermes, the god of hermeneutics, in both the good and evil sense, for, as Socrates warned, Hermes is forever interpreter and thief, messenger and liar, just as the character of Kent in *King Lear* will be shown to be. The resulting crisis, however, has created the need to rethink interpretation in the field of literature, too, in the hope of finding a hermeneutic system capable of standing the test of time.

From the clinical point of view, my opinion as a psychoanalyst is fairly radical: there is no *psychoanalysis*, in the authentic sense of a psychotherapeutic process aimed at restructuring a personality through the discovery of an inner world, other than the one practiced in a *setting* on the basis of timing and methods dictated by the consolidated experience of the psychoanalyst, as well as by the particular needs of individual patients. At the same time, I believe that what is known as applied psychoanalysis has real value as a critical stimulus that, like all human ideas, can be both refuted and perfected.

Having established that psychoanalysis can be a useful critical discipline, I have felt reasonably free to use it in all directions in order to reach different objectives. I mainly intend to deal with characters and events as if they had been real; from the fifth section of this essay onward, I shall also observe them from the point of view of the process by which they were molded. I am aware that some critics are opposed to the application of psychoanalysis or, more generally, of psychology to the study of literature. Suffice it to remember the much lamented Northrop Frye. I must confess, however, that I have never found the arguments presented particularly convincing and shall endeavor not to worry unduly about establishing critical frontiers.

Like many disciplines that have enjoyed the naïve acclaim so often lavished on the new, psychoanalysis needed to be freed from initial, unacknowledged claims to hegemony as well as from a reductionist tendency that is something quite different from the legitimate "genetic" point of view (considered to be its main strength) according to which the complexities of the present arise from the past—a concept neatly expressed in the dictum "the Child is father of the Man." Psychoanalysis should, however, also be freed from what I have previously had occasion to call the danger of tautology, which is part of the hermeneutic circle indicated by Heidegger.

The appeal of reductionism might have tempted me to maintain that I offer *the* keys to an understanding of *Madame Bovary* and *King Lear*. I have been very careful not to do so either implicitly or explicitly and have pointed this out at times when I hoped the reader would be particularly attentive. Great literature, like true poetry, is what it is partly because it is overdetermined: not only does it allow an exploration of different planes by exploiting the richness of meanings, but it also continues to reveal new structures. Not all of these, however, are supporting structures. The works of Flaubert and Shakespeare continue to fascinate us precisely because they give the impression of subtly concealing other structures and meanings. Those commentators who claim to offer the ultimate interpretation of any given work appear to me not only to be ridiculously arrogant but also to limit and offend our notion of beauty itself. Tautology, by contrast, is the most humiliating of all pitfalls, for it makes both the validity and the "truth" of the outcome of any research depend on the extent to which it confirms what we already knew—or thought we knew. The statement by Karl Jaspers that I have chosen as an epigraph for my essay on *Lear* summarizes with extraordinary clarity what I am attempting to say.

If by concentrating attention on the other half of the couple in my essay on *Madame Bovary* I have succeeded in implying that "bovarysme" cannot exist in a pure state, because of the general premise that suffering and tragedy are inextricably woven into the fabric of human relationships, then I have probably succeeded in my first aim. In my analysis of *Lear,* I have sought to demonstrate that this fabric of relationships has its roots in history. The Shakespearean drama of authoritarianism and ingratitude mirrors a phase of transformation that had slow beginnings—a historic change already noticeable in Boccaccio's *Decameron* that would eventually lead to a reformulation in humanistic terms of the relationship between fathers and children. But to what extent does *Lear* reflect this transformation? If this question is also implicitly answered, then I may have achieved my second objective. And yet I shall not be able to claim to have exhausted the "profound human mystery" of which Jaspers speaks.

It is obviously not for me to say how closely I have kept to this premise. What I have attempted to do, however, is to provide psychoanalytic interpretations that are as far as possible compatible with the logic of the uninitiated. In order to do so, I have thought it worthwhile from time to time to sacrifice both the terminological precision and the "clinical" complexity normally involved in the discussion of mental phenomena.

Acknowledgments

Many have supported my obstinacy. Stefano Agosti, Claude Ambroise, Anthony Basini, Roberto Calasso, Patrick Mahony, and Alessandro Serpieri pointed out aspects I had neglected to explore in my research. Anthony Burgess, Michel David, Enzo Siciliano, Stefano Tettamanti, and various psychoanalyst friends each offered extensive comments. Their help was invaluable.

Tommaso Senise—a very important person in my life—has provided a livelier stimulus than the books I have consulted. I am indebted to Cesare Segre and Giuseppe Sertoli for their extremely careful reading of the final draft of the Italian manuscript.

My daughter Dianella, Antony Alexander, Nicolas Barker, Aldo Canevari, Piero Colonna di Paliano, Mark Evrard, and Romano Giachetti have dealt patiently with all my editing requests (and I can be tediously insistent). I owe a particular debt of thanks to Colin Rice. I also wish to express my gratitude to Jill Duncan of the London Institute of Psychoanalysis, to Colin Stevenson, of the London Library, and to his assistant Amanda Robertson, for having supported my research, and to Joan E. Howard for her very thorough copyediting. Loretta Mellina and Maria Teresa Piredda have gathered the scattered jottings of my thoughts with equal patience. Last but not least, my thanks go to my wife, Carmencho, without whose help—in her own words—this book would not have been written.

The King

the Adulteress

For my parents

Charbovari

An Essay on *Madame Bovary*

Not Merely an Imbecile

"Charles et Emma faisaient comme une société particulière."[1] This sentence, which appeared in the autograph version of *Madame Bovary* delivered to the copyist but which was later removed by Flaubert, is fairly representative of the theme of this essay. In order to understand the sentence fully, it will be necessary to unearth and investigate some of the distorted readings that have accompanied the fortunes of this novel.

Stereotypes and prejudices have at least some positive aspects. They help, for example, to attract many insecure souls to art. Unguided by a mediating stereotype, the insecure might not find the courage to explore an unknown territory that is full of pitfalls. Nor should the anxiety involved in expressing an opinion about an established masterpiece be underestimated. Stereotypes, however, are based on collective prejudices and have the advantage not only of ignoring (indeed disguising) the latter but also of providing a sort of blueprint for the conformist response: they reassure us by making us feel that we are in good company.

Stereotypes obviously also have negative aspects: they inhibit readers or spectators and hinder their growth as individuals, just as collective prejudices, as Jung would have said, prevent an individual from becoming himself.[2] There are, however, also some particularly enduring stereotypes that are endowed with the magnetic force of the archetype—these I would be inclined to call "natural." At least one such stereotype is involved in *Madame Bovary,* and at least one other will be seen to be operative in *King Lear.*

The "natural" stereotype I have in mind is one that is handed down unchanged from one generation to the next, one that expects certain characters or situations to fit neatly into a pre-established class, as if they belonged to some sort of botanical species. I have often wondered whether authors themselves might not be at least partly responsible for this type of cliché so often found in literature. I believe this to be true in the case of Flaubert and *Madame Bovary*. By textual manipulation, Flaubert contributed to the creation of at least one stereotype that affects the entire novel (indeed, it is my belief that he also constructed others around this one). This is one of Flaubert's fascinating traits, like his love for Rabelais and Byron because they wrote "with the intention of harming mankind and laughing in his face [dans l'intention de nuire au genre humain et de lui rire à la face]."

A rather curious observation will serve as a starting point: no one doubts that the title *Madame Bovary* refers to the heroine, even though in reality there are three Mesdames Bovary in the novel, but since Emma's presence is as striking as it is compelling, this fact eludes most readers.[3] There are three Mesdames Bovary, then, and yet the densely written opening pages of the novel are devoted to Charles Bovary. By means of carefully selected episodes, Flaubert narrates a sizable part of Charles's life, beginning with his by no means easy childhood. Only for him are we given such a detailed case history. In the case of Emma, Flaubert limits himself to some passing statements about her years at boarding school and other brief observations, such as "When her mother died, she wept a great deal the first few days [Quand sa mère mourut, elle pleura beaucoup les premiers jours]" (30/72).[4]

Why does Flaubert show so much interest in Charbovari? Is this an acceptable paradox, or something else? A warning sign perhaps, or even a key Flaubert wishes to provide us with before we enter the novel? Given that Flaubert himself has directed our attention toward Charles, I would suggest following his lead, at least this once, and leaving aside Emma, who has always been the (perhaps exaggerated) center of attention for both readers and critics. This is not to say that she should be neglected altogether; I am simply suggesting that we should let her pervade us and speak to us with her own voice. While observing her, we should keep a sharp eye on the man she has chosen to marry. I am fairly sure that in this way we may chance upon an Emma Bovary not quite so familiar as the one usually described and accepted by literary critics.

This issue can be left aside for the moment, however. The earliest theorizing—if not the actual coinage of the word "bovarysme"—can be traced back to two psychological essays published by Jules de Gaultier under the title *Bovarysme*.[5] Writing at the turn of the century, de Gaultier may be considered to have been extremely well informed about psychology, a man of great flair, and in some ways a precursor of modern psychological criticism. The "ideological 'bovarysme'" about which he writes represents an attempt to understand the psychology of the individual by concentrating in particular on the gap between dream and reality, pure desire and everyday life. There can be no doubt that Emma repeatedly confirms the existence of such a gap—in the following passage, for instance: "She was in love with Léon, and she sought solitude, the better to take her pleasure, undistracted, in images of him. The actual sight of him upset these voluptuous meditations [Elle était amoureuse de Léon, et elle recherchait la solitude, afin de pouvoir plus à l'aise se délecter en son image, la vue de sa personne troublait la volupté de cette méditation]" (85/141). De Gaultier, who can be credited with having avoided using the moralistic yardstick, succeeded in making "bovarysme" a characteristic common to all Flaubert's characters. He writes: "A weakness in their personality: this is what initially compels all of Flaubert's characters to believe that they are other than they really are. . . . But this weakness in their personality is always linked with some feeling of impotence." He adds: "All of these Flaubertian figures have one point in common. In each of them one can discern traces of conditioning, as if they had been hypnotized into imagining themselves to be other than they really are."[6]

Baudelaire was the first to sense that Emma might be a hysteric. Flaubert replied that such insight had allowed Baudelaire to penetrate "the arcane in the book."[7] When outlining the concept of "bovarysme," de Gaultier described certain characteristics that pertain to hysterics, though he was perhaps not fully aware of doing so. Emma might be seen as one of the prototypes of the hysterical woman, as she was perceived not only in the second half of the nineteenth century but also as she is perceived today, at least by those who can still recognize her symptoms. For thousands of years, hysteria was (mistakenly) considered to be a typically female disorder, an illness that develops without any relation to social environment. Like hysteria, "bovarysme" does not in fact exist in a pure state. The general observation that mental suffering and tragedy are inextricably woven into the fabric of human relationships certainly applies to Emma, Charles, and all the other characters in the novel.

It is on the relationship between Emma and Charles that I wish to dwell, for although Emma's "bovarysme" predates her meeting with Charles, the exceedingly strange bond between them undoubtedly steers it in the direction of tragedy.

The first edition of the novel itself is dedicated to a lawyer, Marie Antoine-Jules Sénard. Former president of the National Assembly and Minister of the Interior, Sénard was a friend of the Flaubert family. Gustave thanks him for "the magnificent speech" that had established his innocence at his trial in the Sixth Correctional Chamber of the Palais de Justice. He had been accused of indecency and of offending public and religious morality. This is what Sénard had to say about Emma's husband in his celebrated speech to the court:

> There is not one man who has read it who would not say, book in hand, that Monsieur Flaubert is not only a great artist but also a compassionate man for the way in which he pours all his horror and contempt upon the woman in the last six pages of the book and reserves all his sympathy for the husband. . . . He does not transform the husband . . . but leaves him exactly as he was right to the end: a good man, common, mediocre, conscious of his professional duties, a man in love with his wife, but sadly lacking in education or lofty thoughts. He remains unchanged even when his wife is on her deathbed. Thus, no other figure is remembered with greater interest. Why? Because he attends to his duties and fulfills them up until the end, while his wife neglects hers.[8]

One cannot but wonder whether Gustave agreed with this portrayal. Sénard belonged to the enlightened bourgeoisie of the

Second Empire but was probably also cynical and not lacking in effrontery.

When the novel appeared, Edmund Texier, a critic writing for *L'Illustration,* was irritated by it and wrote rather irascibly that Charles, a calm individual in love with his wife, had failed to arouse his interest or move him to tears as he should have done. With an inexplicable lack of taste, Flaubert had enjoyed drawing him from the very start as one of those everyday figures whose characteristics refuse to remain in one's memory. Albert Thibaudet took Texier haughtily to task. According to him,[9] Flaubert uses Charles to ridicule goodness; never having harmed anyone, he is the prototype of the imbecile. He is an imbecile in thought, a pavement of commonplaces; he is an imbecile in deed, being incapable of doing anything at all—suffice it to recall the disastrous attempt to straighten the cripple's leg. Charles is blind on three counts: to the wife who betrays him, the chemist who outdoes him professionally, and the lawyers who gnaw away at his property. This paradoxical figure seems almost to have been deliberately constructed as a counterpoint to Emma and is one of the most innovative elements in Flaubert's novel.

When Thibaudet can no longer ignore the fact that Emma is continually and all too easily seduced by her lovers, he concludes that she was unlucky not to have an ordinary husband who was able to satisfy her—the type of man that can, despite the odds, be found. In my opinion he is wrong, although he does show original insight in one sense: Charles Bovary is no ordinary husband. Thibaudet senses this even if he does not go on to draw any conclusions from the fact. For Thibaudet, Charles is the complete opposite of Flaubert, "a nonbeing opposed to his own being."[10] Agreeing with Flaubert, Thibaudet had called Charles "an imbecile," although he could obviously not have imagined that less than forty years later Sartre would repeatedly call *Gustave* an "idiot." I have also enjoyed looking for (and finding) a fair number of historical and psychological circumstances that link Gustave and Charles.

So colorless does Charles seem that many critics, from Auerbach to Lukàcs, have ignored him altogether. Nabokov describes him as "simple-minded," while Félicien Marceau, who is evidently fond of paradoxes, maintains that Emma and Lheureux are the real couple in the novel.[11]

Might all of this point to the presence of a natural stereotype? As I have already suggested, Flaubert endorses these aspects of Charles's personality without attempting to describe or even hint at the depth of Charles's soul through either his words or his actions; he would rather have us accept as truth the occasional piece of information he gives us about him. There is no harm, for example, in having Père Rouault call Bovary a *gringalet,* meaning a slightly comical, insignificant sort of fellow. Similarly, he reveals severe but probably accurate opinions about Charles: his "conversation was as flat as any pavement, everyone's ideas trudging along it in their weekday clothes [la conversation de Charles était plate comme un trottoir de rue, et les idées de tout le monde y défilaient, dans leur costume ordinaire] (31/74). And yet we should not forget a truth that is too often overlooked—the *bêtise* and flatness of all the other characters in the novel. But Flaubert goes even further: he defames Charles Bovary. Let us consider a random example. During one of the hottest spells of summer, the Marquis d'Andervilliers "had had an abscess in his mouth, which Charles had cured quite miraculously, with a nice touch of the lancet [il avait eu un abcès dans la bouche, dont Charles l'avait soulagé comme par miracle, en y donnant à point un coup de lancette]" (35/79). Why should Flaubert have added "quite miraculously"? One feels like asking, What do you know about it? What if Charles were potentially a skillful surgeon as well as a good doctor?

Flaubert, who for many remains the theorist of the writer's impersonality, goes even further; he enters the minds of Charles and Emma and reads their thoughts. When Emma straightens her husband's tie and swaps his faded gloves for another pair, is she really taking care of him? Flaubert assures us that she is prompted by "egotism and nervous vexation [égoisme, agacement nerveux]" (49/95); he uses the same instance to stress that she did all this "*not, as he imagined, for his sake* [my italics] [ce n'était pas, comme il croyait, pour lui]" (48/95). He wishes to influence us. To quote Greimas, he goes from *letting one know* to *making one believe* by introducing elements that tend to limit the interpretations open to the reader. Genette would add more simply that Flaubert is here regulating information by choosing a restrictive point of view.[12]

Flaubert would have us believe that Charles does not understand what is going on right under his nose, just as he does not understand human beings—at least not women. But what if, in some impenetrable corner of his unconscious, Charles did in fact register and comprehend everything? Surely Flaubert should have sensed that perception and will might exist unbeknown to the subject who possesses them. Might not Emma behave that way out of a sense of guilt, because she has ambivalent feelings toward her husband? It is worth bearing in mind that Flaubert himself makes this suggestion on more than one occasion. To give just one example (to which I shall later return): On the evening before the failed attempt to straighten Hippolyte's leg, is it not a fact that Emma begins to feel repentant and goes so far as to wonder "why it was she detested Charles, and whether it wouldn't be better to be able to love him [pourquoi donc elle exécrait Charles, et s'il n'eût pas été meilleur de le pouvoir aimer]" (140/207)? These are typical manifestations of ambivalence and feelings of guilt.

We cannot, then, rely on the judgments that Flaubert, secure in his position as author of the novel, would have us accept. Gustave was a mystifier (a creator of mystery), an able misinformer—though only partly at a conscious level. This assertion should not surprise the reader. It is not possible to go into detail here, but what can be said is that poets—indeed, artists in general—create only *to a certain degree* with the conscious part of their mind. They mainly use the preconscious, a nonconscious part that is able to draw on both reality and the most recondite areas of the unconscious and is capable of synthesis and overdeterminations of which the poor conscious ego is not even remotely aware. Paradoxically then, it might be said that writers are not *totally* aware of the psychology of their own characters—which is obviously of great advantage to the process of artistic creation. This point was underlined by Alberto Moravia in an assertion that, whether it is true or not, is certainly effective: since Freud there have been no more Dostoyevskys.

Jean-Paul Sartre can be credited with being the first critic, possibly the only one, to have written about his bizarre adolescent interest in Charbovari:

> I read the last pages of *Madame Bovary* twenty times; in the end I knew whole paragraphs by heart without being any the wiser about the behavior of the poor widower: he found letters, but was that a good reason for letting his beard grow? He looked sullenly at Rodolphe and must have had a grudge against him, but why, I'd like to know? And why does he say to him: "I don't feel any resentment"? Why did Rodolphe find him "comical and somewhat cowardly"? Then Charles Bovary dies: of a broken heart, of an illness? And why did the doctor perform an autopsy on him when it was all over anyway? I loved that tough resistance that I could never get to the bottom of. Mystified and exhausted though I was, I reveled in the ambiguous pleasure of understanding without understanding.[13]

Young Sartre sensed that everything was yet to be discovered about Charles Bovary; unfortunately, the part of *L'Idiot de la famille* that would have disclosed the secrets contained in these words remained unwritten, and so we shall never know how those early insights would have developed.[14]

In his commentary on *Madame Bovary*, Maurice Bardèche expressed the felicitous insight that the behavior of Léon, Rodolphe, and Emma is consistent with their psychological characteristics. They do not surprise us: "Only in the astonishing figure of Charles Bovary, to whom little justice has yet been done, does Flaubert allow us a glimpse of the unplumbed depths of the soul."[15] This is an invitation to restore dramatic dignity to Charbovari. While it is impossible to assemble all of the pieces of the puzzle that would lead us to a full appreciation of this dignity, consideration can be given to a few brief passages taken from various chapters of the novel.

Is a special effort really required to understand the suffering that must have dogged Charles's childhood and adolescence? Charles is a country lad, a little backward at school, but as sturdy as an oak. He wears blue stockings, yellowish trousers, and a rather unusual cap.

It was one of those hats of the Composite order, in which we find features of the military bear-skin, the Polish chapska, the bowler hat, the beaver and the cotton nightcap, one of those pathetic things, in fact, whose mute ugliness has a profundity of expression like the face of an imbecile. (1–2)

[C'était une de ces coiffures d'ordre composite, où l'on retrouve les éléments du bonnet à poil, du chapska, du chapeau rond, de la casquette de loutre et du bonnet de coton, une de ces pauvres choses, enfin, dont la laideur muette a des profondeurs d'expression comme le visage d'un imbécile.] (36)

This headgear is the cause of his first clash—as far as we know—with his fellow human beings and with authority. It also earns him his first punishment: "As for you, the new boy, you will write out for me twenty times the verb *ridiculus sum* [Quant à vous, le nouveau, vous me copierez vingt fois le verbe *ridiculus sum*]" (3/37). Charbovari causes hilarity among his schoolmates and is obliged to suffer the consequences according to the sensitive pedagogy of his time.

His relationship with his military father amounts to nothing more than superficial contact with "a handsome man, a big talker [un bel homme, hâbleur]" (3/38), a womanizer who reels off vulgar gallantry and is always jingling about in his spurs. Formerly an assistant surgeon in the army, he had been obliged to resign his commission after the discovery of irregularities in the recruitment office. He had then used his physical charms to get his hands on a sixty-thousand-franc dowry, which he had squandered in the space of a few years. Being essentially weak and indecisive, he becomes depressive, "chagrined and remorseful [chagrin, rongé de regrets]" (4/38). He is a difficult person to deal with, and it is impossible for Charles to identify with him.

Charles's mother, by contrast, is blinded by passion and loves her husband "with such servility [avec mille servilités]" (4/38) that she ends up by estranging him even further. Indeed, this kind of submissiveness obtains the opposite of what it seeks. At first, she silently suffers her husband's affairs, his drunkenness, and his visits to the brothel. Then her pride causes her to react. She withdraws behind a wall of stubborn silence, "swallowing down her rage in a mute stoicism that she kept until her death [avalant sa rage dans un stoïcisme muet, qu'elle garda jusqu'à sa mort]" (4/38). She behaves like this toward her husband. Charles is the object of totally different feelings.

In the best bourgeois tradition of the time, when the child was born he was taken from his mother and handed over to a wet nurse: "Once he came home, the little lad was treated like a prince [Rentré chez eux, le marmot fut gâté comme un prince]" (4/38). The mother who had not breast-fed him now fed him jam. His father, on the contrary, had a rather manly attitude toward infancy and favored a Spartan upbringing for the child so that he would develop a robust constitution: "He sent him to bed without a fire, taught him to take great swigs of rum and to shout insults at religious processions [Il l'envoyait se coucher sans feu, lui apprenait à boire de grands coups de rhum et à insulter les processions]" (4/39). But the little boy has a gentle nature and is not responsive to his father's efforts. It is his mother who seduces him by cutting out paper figures for him, telling him stories, and amusing him with endless monologues full of melancholy cheerfulness and cajolery.

Living in such isolation, she shifted on to this childish head all her scattered and broken vanities. She dreamed of high office, she already saw him, tall, handsome, talented, established, an engineer or a magistrate. (5)

[Dans l'isolement de sa vie, elle reporta sur cette tête d'enfant toutes ses vanités éparses, brisées. Elle rêvait de hautes positions, elle le voyait déjà grand, beau, spirituel, établi, dans les ponts et chaussées ou dans la magistrature.] (39)

In this way Charles becomes the receptacle of his mother's narcissistic dreams, a mere appendage. Any of us would suffer inhibitions and pain if we were fed, day in and day out, on our mother's resentment, her disappointments, her unhealthy desire for revenge, without a mediating father to offer a more disinterested and constructive love. And what resentment we would feel toward such parents!

Flaubert tells us, however, that Charles was "a boy of sober temperament, who played at play-time, worked in school hours, listened in class, slept well in the dormitory, ate well in the refec-

tory [un garçon de tempérament modéré, qui jouait aux recré-
ations, travaillait à l'étude, écoutant en classe, dormant bien au
dortoir, mangeant bien au réfectoire]" (6/40). Again, this seems
to suggest two possible interpretations: either the meekness he
displayed was not altogether authentic, or else Charles, compared to ordinary mortals, was made of totally different, rather
exceptional stuff. Of course, young Bovary's weaknesses soon
begin to show and he faces his first existential crises: he grows
thinner and taller and his face takes on a mournful look that
makes it almost interesting. Little by little, a sort of innate indo-
lence leads him to discard all his fine intentions. One day he
misses drill, the next he fails to turn up for lessons, and then he
begins to wallow in his laziness until he finally gives up going to
school altogether. His passion for dominoes grows and he spends
all his evenings in dingy taverns.

No longer tied to his mother's apron strings, Charles takes up
gambling, from which he derives an almost sensual joy: it is as
though he wanted to give meaning to his life by trusting in
fortune rather than in his personal resources. He discovers love
and shows a keen interest, for example, in Béranger, the poet who
sings of the sufferings of the common people. He even earns an
honorable mention in natural history, but "he totally failed his
Public Health Officer's examination [il échoua complètement à
son examen d'officier de santé]" (7/42). Would it be too much to
suspect that this misfortune is symptomatic of a subtle but nevertheless extraordinary failure neurosis?

They were expecting him at home that same evening to celebrate his success! He set off on foot and stopped just outside the village, where he sent for
his mother, and told her everything. She made excuses for him, blaming his
failure on the injustice of the examiners, and reassured him, promising to
sort it out. Only five years later did Monsieur Bovary learn the truth; it was
ancient history, he accepted it, unable in any case to imagine that any son of
his could be a clot. (7–8)

[On l'attendait le soir même à la maison pour fêter son succès. Il partit à
pied et s'arrêta vers l'entrée du village, où il fit demander sa mère, lui conta
tout. Elle l'excusa, rejetant l'échec sur l'injustice des examinateurs, et le
raffermit un peu, se chargeant d'arranger les choses. Cinq ans plus tard

seulement, M. Bovary connut la vérité; elle était vieille, il l'accepta, ne pouvant d'ailleurs supposer qu'un homme issu de lui fût un sot.] (42–43)

His mother protects him; she refuses to accept his inability, puts everything right, and excludes Charles's father from the matter. Probably overcome by fatigue, the father ends up quietly acquiescing in his wife's decisions. Until now, Charles has always found a substitute for security in this maternal protectiveness, which has given him a false sense of self-importance, but his failure of the examination—in which he later manages to get "quite a decent pass [une assez bonne note]" (8/43)—points to his tendency to play the killjoy.

His mother even finds him a wife, who is "ugly, thin as a rake and splendidly bepimpled [laide, sèche comme un cotret, et bourgeonné [*sic*] comme un printemps]" (8/43), and it is she who will wear the trousers. Although Charles does not rebel, he will never love her. Why must he always offer drinks to anyone who comes to call? How stubborn of him not to agree to wear a woolen vest! He really should not eat quite so much. Like a pair of sharpened knives, the two women enjoy scarifying him "with their remarks and their criticisms [par leurs réflexions et leurs observations]" (14/51). Flaubert's choice of the verb "scarifier" is particularly evocative, almost as if Charles's skin were being prepared with superficial incisions for the application of a leech.

Considering the cold precision with which Flaubert describes Charles's youth, it is natural to wonder once again whether these events might not have had some repercussion on the nature of Emma's future husband, on his chances of being happy with the woman with whom he had fallen in love. After all, he is truly in love with Emma, as his first wife notices immediately: so that is why he comes home looking so cheerful after visiting her!

According to the country custom, she offered him something to drink. He refused, she insisted, and in the end asked him, laughingly, to have a glass of liqueur with her. So she went to the cupboard for a bottle of curaçao, reached down two little glasses, filled one right to the brim, poured only a drop into the other, and, after clinking glasses, raised it to her lips. As it was almost empty, she had to drink it from below; and, with her head right back, her lips pushed out, her neck stretching, she laughed at getting nothing, while the tip of her tongue, from between perfect teeth, licked delicately over the bottom of the glass. (17)

[Selon la mode de la campagne, elle lui proposa de boire quelque chose. Il refusa, elle insista, et enfin lui offrit, en riant, de prendre un verre de liqueur avec elle. Elle alla donc chercher dans l'armoire un verre de curaçao, atteignit deux petits verres, emplit l'un jusqu'au bord, versa à peine dans l'autre, et, après avoir trinqué, le porta à sa bouche. Comme il était presque vide, elle se renversait pour boire; et, la tête en arrière, les lèvres avancées, le cou tendu, elle riait de ne rien sentir, tandis que le bout de sa langue, passant entre ses dents fines, léchait à petits coups le fond du verre.] (55)

According to some critics, Madame Bovary and what has traditionally become known as "bovarysme" begin here, with the implication that sensuality is necessarily the mark of an adulterous and unsatisfied woman (a prejudice that Denis de Rougemont would call romantic). This vision of Emma, which affects Charles so deeply, already contains the elements of their tragedy: he falls in love because the bourgeois peasant girl is uninhibited and more or less offers herself to him. And yet, when the scene is tinged with the young man's deepest anxieties, the same girl can turn into a greedy woman, an insatiable phantom who drains the glass to the very last drop. Charles is attracted by this voraciousness and subsequently exploits it.

Soon after his wife's death, he uses Père Rouault as a go-between to ask for Emma's hand in marriage. Rouault asks his daughter what she thinks and informs his future son-in-law in the agreed manner. That was undoubtedly the way such things were done in those days.

But He Is Fast Asleep!

In the days of Madame Dubuc, Charles's first wife, Charles's mother had felt that she was still her son's favorite. She had found him a spotty wife and could continue to reign supreme; now she sees Charles's love for Emma as an act of betrayal and, at the same time, an encroachment on her own private property. As she observes her son's happiness, she feels as sad as "a ruined man gazing in, through the window, at the people dining in his old house [comme quelqu'un de ruiné, qui regarde, à travers les carreaux, des gens attablés dans son ancienne maison]." Yet she does not show resignation but reminds him of "her troubles and her sacrifices" [ses peines et ses sacrifices"] (33/76); comparing her own situation to Emma's neglectfulness, she concludes that it is not reasonable for her son to adore his wife to the exclusion of everyone else. Charles's mother seeks self-fulfillment through her son and expects him to achieve great things, but when he shows that he has a mind of his own, she scorns him. This meddling creates a conflict in Charles between his feelings for the woman he loves and a strong bond over which he has no control: "he respected his mother, and he loved his wife immensely; the judgement of the one he considered infallible, and yet he found the other irreproachable [il respectait sa mère, et il aimait infiniment sa femme; il considérait le jugement de l'une comme infaillible, et cependant il trouvait l'autre irréprochable]" (33/77). It is a decisive moment. Charles does not find the strength to cut the umbilical cord and is forced into a compromise that ruins his marriage and the love of his life.

At one point, Emma talks to Félicité about her problems and tells her that they began after she had married ["c'est après le mariage que ça m'est venu"] (143). Though thinking along mistaken lines, she vaguely senses the extent to which Charles has catalyzed her tragedy and goes so far as to think that her husband is to blame for all of her troubles. As always happens in these cases, Emma has forgotten that when Charles visited Les Bertaux for the first time she was already profoundly disappointed, thinking that there was nothing more to learn, nothing worth the effort of emotion. In other words, she was suffering from the sort of melancholy that, like all "existential" melancholy, has its origins in the remote past. Charles does nothing more than enter her existing state of depression. Unable to rely on her spontaneity, on an authentic inner joy, Emma at first tries ingenuously to invent love according to the theories she had been brought up on.

Even Maître Sénard pointed out at the trial that Emma does

not admit defeat. In the moonlit garden, she recites passionate poetry to Charles and softly sings melancholy airs to him; "but she found herself just as calm afterwards as she had been before, and Charles seemed neither more amorous nor more excited [mais elle se trouvait ensuite aussi calme qu'auparavant, et Charles n'en paraissait ni plus amoureux ni plus remu]" (33/77). In the end she comes to the conclusion that his passion is by no means excessive. His expressions of affection become as regular as clockwork: "he embraced her at the same time every day [il l'embrassait à de certaines heures]." Giving her a kiss is just another prosaic habit, "a favourite pudding after the monotony of dinner [comme un dessert prévu d'avance, après la monotonie du dîner]" (34/77). Charles puts on his slippers and Flaubert introduces a dreary gastronomic simile, which marks the beginning of an irreversible decline. Emma is already alone.

It is at the château of the Marquis d'Andervilliers that Emma turns into Madame Bovary, when committing her first act of revenge. Charles, who has put respect for his mother's infallibility before Emma's love, sees her in her new saffron-colored dress and comes to kiss her on the shoulder. He is aroused, but Emma's pride is hurt and she gives vent to all the bitterness that has been building up: "'Leave me alone,' she said, 'you're creasing my dress!' ['Laisse-moi,' dit-elle, 'tu me chiffonnes!']" (39/83). She then concedes a waltz to the Viscount:

Passing near the doors, Emma's dress, at the hem, caught on his trousers; their legs entwined; he looked down at her, she looked up at him. (41)

[En passant auprès des portes, la robe d'Emma, par le bas, s'ériflait au pantalon; leurs jambes entraînaient l'une dans l'autre; il baissait ses regards vers elle, elle levait les siens vers lui.] (86)

And what does Charles do? He spends a full five hours watching a game of whist "without understanding a thing [sans y rien comprendre]" (42/86). Now five hours is a suspiciously long time. Surely this entitles us to wonder whether Charles was really watching the players or was lost in his own thoughts.

Although this rather disturbing clue is probably not enough to dismantle commonplace ideas about Bovary, it may well cause the reader to reflect. All these clichés about Bovary seem to have the mysterious ability to engender a plethora of foolish consequences. In his (sadly unsuccessful) film version of *Madame Bovary,* with Isabelle Huppert in the leading role, Claude Chabrol not only adopts the traditional approach to Charles but even compounds it with a show of bad taste that must have caused a shudder in all those admirers of Flaubert who had rashly trusted in the reputation of an otherwise great director. In the scene of the ball in the castle, Chabrol dispels all possible doubts about Bovary's clumsy imbecility by having a liveried servant offer him champagne from a tray. "Dom Pérignon," remarks the servant (as probably still happens in the castles frequented by Chabrol). And how does Charles respond? He introduces himself: "Bovary."

Charles's indifference to that first act of unfaithfulness troubles Emma, who perhaps wants to make up for it before it is too late: "She took off her clothes and she curled up [with Charles] in between the sheets [Elle se déshabilla et se blottit entre les draps, contre Charles]" (42/87) . . . But he is fast asleep!

The next morning, when they are leaving in their gig, they are overtaken by some gentlemen on horseback coming from the Château de Vaubyessard "with cigars in their mouths [avec des cigares à la bouche]." While Charles is adjusting the horse's girth with some string, he sees a cigar case "edged in green silk with a coat-of-arms at the centre [tout bordé de soie vert et blasonné]" and picks it up. " 'There's even a couple of cigars in it,' he said, 'just right for tonight, after dinner' ['Il y a même deux cigares dedans,' dit-il; 'ce sera pour ce soir après dîner']" (43/88).

Bovary is the sort of man who contents himself with the leftovers (and thus makes Emma feel like one); he adopts manly attitudes with someone else's cigar in his mouth; Charles makes himself look ridiculous through pretending to be what he is not. It is the recurrent pattern once again. But while this had only caused his schoolmates and the teacher to laugh at him, Emma's pride is hurt to such an extent that she loses her temper with Nastasie, the maid, and dismisses her. That the true target of her anger is Charles (or perhaps the mother-in-law who has castrated her husband) is clear from what she says when she sees him, a nonsmoker, smoking one of the notorious cigars. Adopting a scornful motherly tone, she tells him: " 'You'll make yourself ill' ['Tu vas te faire mal']" (43/89).

Charles picks up other people's cigars and smokes them; he expresses his feelings like clockwork. He annoys Emma by kissing her like a petulant child and turns his back on her while she dances in the Viscount's arms (he is not interested in whist and does not even know how to play it). Charles does not have "an ounce of ambition [point d'ambition]" (48/94); he is innocent and unprepossessing. Rodolphe immediately notices that he is unshaven and has dirty fingernails, which can only be taken as an all-clear sign by an expert lady-killer.

A doctor from Yvetot publicly humiliates him during a consultation, and when Charles tells the story to Emma that same evening (one wonders why he did not just keep quiet and save face like any ordinary mortal), she is furious with her husband's colleague. This moves Charles to kiss Emma's forehead tearfully. What effect does this have on Emma? "[S]he was boiling with shame, she wanted to hit him, she went out to the passage to open the window, and breathe the fresh air to calm herself [elle était exaspérée de honte, elle avait envie de le battre, elle alla dans le corridor ouvrir la fenêtre et huma l'air frais pour se calmer]" (48/95).

Charles irritates Emma precisely when he becomes affectionate. It is as though he had a talent for always misunderstanding the true reasons behind Emma's reactions. This should not be so surprising, if he is such a dullard. But Charles actually shows perfect timing in exploiting such misunderstandings in order to increase Emma's irritation—a singular way for a blockhead to behave. A number of episodes will be seen to confirm this repeated and therefore suspicious behavior.

Emma, then, is increasingly annoyed by Charles's behavior.

As he got older, he seemed to be getting coarser in his ways; during dessert, he used to cut bits off the corks from the empty bottles; after meals, he used to suck his teeth; eating his soup, he made a gurgling noise with every mouthful. (48)

[Il prenait, avec l'âge, des allures épaisses; il coupait, au dessert, le bouchon des bouteilles vides; il se passait, après manger, la langue sur les dents; il faisait, en avalant sa soupe, un gloussement à chaque gorgée.] (95)

As a result, out of simple irritation, Emma goes back to her premarital state of depression, which is now accentuated. She abandons her music, her piano, her drawing, her sewing—the only interests that bourgeois society allows a woman, who is brought up to become mistress of a household, to breed and be a *remedium concupiscentiae*. All that is left to her is to yield to the compromise offered by neurosis. She grows pale and suffers from palpitations. Charles treats her with valerian oil and camphor baths. Emma develops a dry cough and loses her appetite completely. The time has come for a change of air.

Charles's silent rancor takes on the subtlest form of which it is capable—self-sacrifice. He leaves Tostes "just when he was beginning to get on [où il commençait à s'y poser]" (53/100) and moves to Yonville. It is as if he were saying, Do you see how much I love you? I'm even prepared to ruin my career. How do you intend to show me your gratitude? This technique of masochistic aggression will be seen again after Charles's failure to straighten the cripple's limb and at the climax of the tragedy.

Meanwhile, like all of those ill-assorted couples who will not or cannot solve their problems in any other way, Charles and Emma reinforce their social and religious contract with a bonding act of *responsibility*. They bring a child into the world.[16]

The Art of Irritating

Charles Bovary acquires extraordinary dramatic force only if we stop seeing him as a passive, blind victim and instead accept the hypothesis that he is a moral masochist, arguably the most accomplished masochist ever to appear in literature. What is deceptive about Charles—indeed, what deceives Charles himself—is that he is apparently a poor soul who, rather surprisingly, is not very suspicious. Most deceptive of all is his very goodness, his simplicity, his imbecility when he needs to act, his blindness in the midst of all the misfortunes that beset him. The untrained eye will not recognize the signs of an inner conflict that has transformed brooding hatred and desire for revenge into dedication and total self-sacrifice or the morbid voyeurism that is transformed into blindness. Only the indirect results of the original conflict manifest themselves, the most striking of these being Emma's decline from irritation into suicidal despair.

Emma's symptoms are quite transparent. Homais, for example, understands everything: as her palpitations possibly mimic her desire for love, so her nervous cough conceivably expresses her wish to unleash all her pent-up anger against Charles.

Bovary's symptoms, however, are not transparent.[17] It is as though he is protecting himself from what is seething inside him and from life's misfortunes by wearing a suit of armor made up of defensive character traits that transform his sadism into masochism. Yet from time to time the violence of his sadism manages to force its way out through the chinks in this armor. For instance, when Emma first enters the bedroom on her wedding night, what should she see but an object that revives her fears of being compared with Charles's first wife. He has *forgotten* to remove his first wife's wedding bouquet. And when Léon leaves Emma to go to Paris, Charles seems to show an anxiety that is almost paternal: "'Poor Léon! . . . How is he going to get on in Paris?' ['Ce pauvre Léon! . . . comment va-t-il vivre à Paris?']" (97/155). Homais, the apothecary, imagines him having great fun but then consoles himself with the thought this would require more money than Léon has at his disposal. Bovary, on the other hand, looks on the black side, thinking above all about the illnesses and the typhoid commonly contracted by students from the provinces. This is not just a casual thought but the manifestation of a deep-seated desire with which he also strikes at his wife—and Emma does in fact shudder ["Emma tressaillit"] (155).

When Rodolphe Boulanger's employee is having his blood let and is in need of assurance, he exclaims: "'Really red is my blood! That must be a good sign, don't you think?' ['Comme j'ai le sang rouge! ce doit être bon signe, n'est-ce pas?']." But Charles com-

ments like a prophet of doom: "'Sometimes . . . they feel nothing at first, then the syncope occurs, especially in well-built
chaps, like this one here' ['Quelquefois . . . l'on n'éprouve rien au
commencement, puis la syncope se déclare, et plus particulière-
ment chez les gens bien constitués, comme celui-ci']" (102/162).
These are all small signs, unconscious concessions that escape the
notice of Emma and the citizens of Yonville l'Abbaye, as well as
that of many others.

It is not long before everybody realizes that Madame Bovary is
compromising her reputation with Léon—everybody, that is, except Charles, "who, not a jealous man, was unsurprised" by their
friendship ["qui, peu jaloux, ne s'en étonnait pas"] (79/133). During the visit to the new textile mill in the valley, Emma and Léon
are ominously together again, with Homais acting as chaperone.
Charles is also present:

He had his cap pulled down to his eyebrows, and his thick lips were trembling, adding a touch of stupidity to his face; even his back, his tranquil
back, was irritating to behold, and in the very look of his coat she found all
the banality of the man. (81)

[Il avait sa casquette enfoncée sur ses sourcils, et ses deux grosses lèvres
tremblotaient, ce qui ajoutait à son visage quelque chose de stupide; son dos
même, son dos tranquille, était irritant à voir, et elle y trouvait étalée sur la
redingote toute la platitude du personnage.] (135–36)

Charles turns his back and sees nothing, as he had at the château, where he had spent five hours at the whist table. Nevertheless, his lips are trembling—a sure sign of conflict. It is Flaubert
himself who reminds us, when describing the tense relationship
between Charles's mother and Emma, that lips tremble out of repressed rage and in an effort to appear kind and civilized. Furthermore, surely Charles's silence and that irritating back of his
are reminiscent of the "mute stoicism" with which his mother expressed her hatred for her husband. This time, however, Charles
provokes a different reaction, for Emma looks at him, "savouring
in her irritation a kind of voluptuous depravity [goûtant ainsi
dans son irritation une sorte de volupté dépravée]" (81/136). The

sadomasochistic tie acquires a thrill of perversion that shows Emma to be a willing accomplice. There will soon be occasion to return to the subject of triangular relationships and the Bovarys.

Emma does make one more attempt to conform to what she believes to be the ideals of her husband: she dedicates herself to looking after the house, takes the baby away from the nurse, and makes sure that Charles's slippers are warming by the fire when he comes home. She is admired by the neighbors for her thriftiness, by Charles's patients for her kindness, and by the poor for her charity. She appeals to her own sense of pride and tells herself that she is virtuous, showing the same naïveté with which she later admits to herself that she has a lover. But her rejected and scorned femininity eventually cause her to rebel: "she was filled with lust, with rage, with hatred [elle était pleine de convoitises, de rage, de haine]" (85/141).

She then falls in love with Léon. But is her love genuine, or is this just one last attempt to arouse Charles's jealousy, to make him love her? Is Emma really only held back by laziness, fear, and modesty as Flaubert gives us to believe? How else can one explain the fact that Charles still has the power to exasperate her? Not even she is aware of how much she cares for her husband. Does she love him? He has never given her the opportunity. His belief that he makes her happy is certainly taken as an insult by her, just as his self-assuredness is taken as a sign of ingratitude.

The sense of impotence that Emma surely feels whenever she attempts to seduce her husband may well, besides hurting her, cause her to doubt her own femininity and destroy her self-confidence. Indeed, her growing hatred for Charles may bespeak a certain genuineness: she wants to be loved and feel like a woman. Emma has certainly married not only Bovary the man (whom she hardly knows) but also Bovary the general practitioner, a figure of some standing in everybody's eyes and socially much more attractive to Emma than Père Rouault, who is a simple farmer. For Emma marriage should automatically combine the two sides of her romantic ideal: it should be able to satisfy her sexual and emotional needs and also create a position on the bourgeois social ladder. The possibility of repudiating her peasant origins, which had been inculcated by the middle-class education she had received, now seems to become a necessity for her. When she realizes that her expectations are being thwarted, Emma does everything she can to force reality into conforming with her ideals.

What gives Emma the vitality that her husband lacks is that, unlike him, she does not surrender: she makes mistakes, she takes risks and attempts to break free from mediocrity. If it is true, as Edmund Wilson maintains, that a romantic is always a rebel, then Emma is both romantic and rebellious. Returning to "bovarysme," Emma's sin is that she confuses reality and imagination in her girlish mind and has no clear idea about the sort of man who might be able to satisfy her. The Viscount fascinates her, but this is probably because of his social status: she is swept away by the embodiment of an enduring image from her childhood. In fact, the Viscount gives the impression of being less valid as a man than Charles, whose patients are very devoted to him (and to whom Père Rouault is surely grateful). Emma is not capable of understanding her husband's complex ambivalence; she certainly does not understand the extent to which Charles's long-standing grudge against his possessive mother poisons his love for his wife and, above all, how much she herself needs someone to hate, someone who can make her suffer. All of this brings us back to the morbid relationship that binds the couple not only to each other but also to Emma's lovers.

It seems natural to return to Flaubert at this stage. It is worth bearing in mind that since the poet or the writer is not fully aware of the psychology of his characters he cannot be totally conscious of the overdetermination that informs his own words—at most he might be conscious of certain aspects or echoes. One of the models for the character of Charles Bovary is in fact thought to have been a certain Roger de Genettes. Flaubert wrote to Louise Colet on 23 December 1853: "I have just seen Père Roger in his frock coat walking down the street with his dog. Poor man! . . . How little he suspects! Have you ever thought of the number of women who have lovers, of all those men with mistresses, of all those relationships hidden behind other relationships? How much lying it involves! What manoeuvring and treachery, what tears, what anguish! [J'ai bien vu le père Roger passer dans la rue avec sa redingote et son chien. Pauvre homme! Comme il se doute peu! As-tu songé quelquefois à cette quantité de femmes qui ont des amants, à ces quantités d'hommes qui ont des maî-tresses, à tous ces ménages sous les autres ménages? Que de mensonges cela suppose! Que de manoeuvres et de trahisons, et de larmes et d'angoisses!]"[18]

More than passing attention should be paid to the episode in which Rodolphe Boulanger offers to help combat Emma's dole-fulness by going horseback riding with her. Emma is reticent, but Charles refuses to miss an opportunity: "'Certainly! Excel-lent. . . . perfect! . . . There's an idea! You should follow it up' ['Certes! Excellent, parfait! . . . Voilà une idée! Tu devrais la suivre]." Emma is forced to accept. "She made a sulky face, gave every kind of excuse, and in the end declared that *it might look rather odd* [Elle prit un air boudeur, chercha mille excuses, et déclara finalement que *cela peut-être semblerait drôle*]." It might well look odd, but this is exactly what Charles wanted. "'I really don't care how it looks' ['Ah, je m'en moque pas mal!'']," he said, spinning round. "'Health comes first! You are making a real mistake!' ['La santé avant tout! Tu as tort!']" (126/191). This scene provides a good illustration of Charles's masochistic technique, taking us back through the years to wonder whether Charbovari really was totally unaware of the fact that his mother's broken dreams and that horribly composite hat of his were responsible for the ridicule heaped on him in the classroom.

To return to the theme of relationships hidden behind other relationships, the *ménages* beneath other *ménages,* the beginning of the horseback riding episode has a sequel that is very interest-ing in this context and obliges us to make a few linguistic reflec-tions. Charles buys his wife a riding habit and *at this point* he writes a letter to Boulanger. Flaubert gives us only an *indirect* account of this letter, although it will be seen that there is actually another indirect version of it. The first of these appears in the first edition of *Madame Bovary.*[19] Here, Charles writes to Bou-langer "that his wife was at his disposal and that they were counting on his kindness [que sa femme était à sa disposition, et qu'ils comptaient sur sa complaisance]" (126/191). This sentence raises the (half-serious) problem of so-called pronominal references: to whom do the pronouns and possessive adjectives refer? We solve the confusion that might normally arise in such cases—and quite spontaneously in everyday discourse—by allowing ourselves to be guided by the context, for it is the context that identifies the persons and objects to which the pronouns and other discourse markers in a sentence actually refer. But in this way the deepest ambiguities, rather than those that are immediately perceptible, might be lost. And in a novel there can be more than one context.

In the context of their unconscious sadomasochistic relationship, Charles seems almost to *push* Emma into the arms of her lovers in order to make her feel increasingly guilty and remain a prey to depression, and Emma, who is still attached to her husband, accepts this.

The letter written by Charles requires further consideration. Flaubert reports Charles as having told Rodolphe "que sa femme était à sa disposition, et qu'ils comptaient sur sa complaisance." If we try to recover the direct version and its context, using something more than mere common sense, the sentence begins to reveal unsuspected meanings. Charles must have written more or less: "Dear Monsieur Boulanger. . . . my wife is at your disposal. We are counting on your kindness" (the commonsense version). The simple fact that he puts his wife at another man's disposal could of itself cause an ironic reaction in those who consider Charles a simpleton, albeit a well-mannered one. But the word "complaisance" that follows adds something more. In French, as in old-fashioned literary English (and in the Italian "compiacenza"), the word implies a wish to be courteous, to render a service, but it also implies self-indulgence—in which there is no clear boundary between *amour propre* and vanity (an attitude wholly appropriate to a cynical seducer).

"Complaisance" also describes an action intended to please someone else. Finally, there is a possible pejorative meaning, which suggests a concession made in order to be kind but not necessarily truthful.[20] Such a definition would seem to leave the way open to lying, which (once accepted) becomes complicity. The word, then, certainly leaves room for a great deal of ambiguity.

It would be worthwhile to consider some of the possible meanings of Charles's words ("que sa femme était à sa disposition, et qu'ils comptaient sur sa complaisance"), which potentially contain a truly remarkable variety of triangulations. Only a few are suggested here, although the inquisitive reader might wish to look for others. They are all arbitrary, but they are theoretically possible because of the ambiguity of the personal pronouns and possessive adjectives used by Flaubert:

Dear Monsieur Boulanger,

. . . my wife is at your disposal and we (Charles and Emma) count on your complaisance;

. . . my wife is at your disposal and you (Emma and Rodolphe) can count on your (Rodolphe's) complaisance;

. . . my wife is at your disposal and you (Emma and Rodolphe) can count on my (Charles's) complaisance;

. . . my wife is at her own disposal . . . ;

. . . my wife is at my disposal . . .

to which can be added all the other possible variants. The last version would correspond, inter alia, to my hypothesis that Charles (albeit with his wife's "consent") plays cat and mouse with Emma's life.

However, another indirect version of the letter exists in a variation written by Flaubert himself: it appears, for example, in the Quentin edition of 1885 and the Conrad edition of 1910.[21] Here we find "que sa femme était à sa disposition, et qu'il comptait sur sa complaisance" (no longer in the third person plural). At this point further tempting interpretations of the second half of the sentence come to mind:

. . . my wife is at your disposal and I count on your complaisance;

. . . my wife is at your disposal and you can count on her complaisance . . .

and so on.

This multifarious play on equivocal relationships could lead to the hidden depths of Gustave's unconscious, to his own relationships and morbidity. Flaubert's entire oeuvre, from the *Correspondance* to *Voyage en Orient*, is shot through with suggestions that seem to support Maurice Bardèche's observation that "the way in which Flaubert's cynicism is transformed into Flaubert's 'humanity' in his novels is a truly miraculous accomplishment."[22]

How to Avoid Gangrene

The episode concerning Bovary's failure to straighten the cripple's limb provides details that further our understanding of the nature—or, rather, the dynamics—of the relationship that binds Charles and Emma to the very end. It also raises the suspicion that, in allowing himself to be persuaded to undertake the operation, Bovary may in fact be both ambitious (though Flaubert says that he is not) and unscrupulous.

The nature of the couple's relationship reminds us that Charles was *not* apathetic by nature or incapable of demonstrating affection and tenderness. This we learn during Emma's pregnancy, for on that occasion his happiness knew no bounds:

he would get up, embrace her, stroke her face, call her little mummy, try to make her dance, and murmur with tears and smiles together, the various fond absurdities that came into his head. The thought of having impregnated her was delectable to him. (70)

[il se levait, il l'embrassait, passait ses mains sur sa figure, l'appelait petite maman, voulait la faire danser, et débitait, maitié riant, moitié pleurant, toutes sortes de plaisanteries caressantes qui lui venaient à l'esprit. L'idée d'avoir engendré le délectait.] (122)

Charles not only feels the urge to destroy his wife but he also loves her deeply. According to the theory I am attempting to outline, he might well unconsciously sense that Rodolphe is no Léon and that he risks losing Emma to him forever. Healing Hippolyte could offer him the chance to win back her affection, which is just what Emma has been waiting for: "how satisfying for her to have coaxed him into taking a step that would enhance his reputation and increase his income. She only wanted to lean upon something more solid than love [quelle satisfaction pour elle que de l'avoir engagé à une démarche d'où sa réputation et sa fortune se trouveraient accrues! Elle ne demandait qu'à s'appuyer sur quelque chose de plus solide que l'amour]" (140/208). Could it be that little Madame Bovary is also a social climber? Perhaps she is, but she is also a woman who is wounded and in search of support for her fragility, in need of something solid to lean on: "She found herself happily revived in a new sentiment, healthier, better, happy to feel some tenderness for this poor boy who so adored her [Elle se trouvait heureuse de se refraîchir dans un sentiment nouveau, plus sain, meilleur, enfin d'éprouver quelque tendresse pour ce pauvre garçon qui la chérissait]" (143/211).

She urges him on and wants him to redeem himself. In the meantime, Charles envisages the fame and increased well-being that (according to our hypothesis) would prevent Emma from deserting him. She turns her attention back to her husband: "The image of Rodolphe passed, fleetingly, through her mind; but her eyes came back to rest upon her Charles; she even noticed to her surprise that his teeth were not too bad at all [L'idée de Rodolphe, un moment, lui passa par la tête, mais ses yeux se reportèrent sur Charles: elle remarqua même avec surprise qu'il n'avait point les dents vilaines]" (143/211). These words are extremely relevant to our "theory," for they show that even the physical interest that Charles arouses is dependent on his behaving in accordance with his wife's expectations. But Bovary cannot have Emma.

What makes Charles a moral masochist is his unconscious belief (a conviction perhaps as old as humanity itself) that renunciation constitutes the only efficient defense against calamity. If he must suffer solitude and despair, then they must be caused by him. He will be the one who orchestrates and manipulates the possibilities of being abandoned—thus turning from potential victim into hidden, supreme controller. In order to bring about this metamorphosis, he creates situations that lead to failure and consequent rejection. The destructiveness he fosters makes him unconsciously feel evil and therefore guilty. Since this might lead to his being abandoned by those who love him, his only defense is to turn himself into a victim.

It is Homais who first suggests performing the operation:

He had just lately read a panegyric on a new method for the cure of club-foot; and as a partisan of progress, he now conceived the patriotic notion that Yonville, *to keep up with the times,* ought to have operations for talipes. "Because," he said to Emma, "what do we risk? Merely consider (and he counted off on his fingers the advantages of this experiment): success almost certain, alleviation and rehabilitation for the patient, rapid and easy fame for the surgeon. Your husband, for example, why should he not relieve poor old Hippolyte from the Golden Lion?" (140)

[Il avait lu dernièrement l'éloge d'une nouvelle méthode pour la cure des pieds bots, et comme il était partisan du progrès, il conçut cette idée patriotique que Yonville, pour se mettre à niveau, devait avoir des opérations de strephopodie. "Car," disait-il à Emma "que risque-t-on? Examinez" (et il énumérait, sur ses doigts, les avantages de la tentative): "succès presque certain, soulagement et embellissement du malade, célébrité vite acquise à l'opérateur. Pourquoi votre mari, par exemple, ne voudrait-il pas débarrasser ce pauvre Hippolyte, du Lion d'Or?"] (208)

Charles allows himself to be tempted, but he operates with a lack of skill that is something much more than suspicious. The reader needs to pay particular attention to the passage in which, with the surgical realism familiar to his most avid readers, Flaubert seems to suggest certainty rather than vague doubt—the certainty that Charles treats his guinea pig with deliberate sadism:

Taking a great many precautions, so as not to disturb the position of the limb, the box was duly removed, and they saw a horrible sight. The shape of the foot was disappearing into a swelling, so gross that the entire skin seemed ready to burst open, and it was covered with patches of bruising inflicted by the famous machine. Hippolyte had already complained that it hurt; nobody had listened; they had to admit that he had not been completely wrong and they let him free for a few hours. But hardly had the oedema gone down a little, than the two men of science thought fit to reinstall the limb in the apparatus, clamping it on even tighter, to hasten the whole process. (144)

[Avec beaucoup de précautions, pour ne pas déranger la position du membre, on retira la boîte, et l'on vit un spectacle affreux. Les formes du pied disparaissaient dans une telle bouffissure que la peau toute entière semblait près de se rompre, et elle était couverte d'ecchymoses occasionnées par la fameuse machine. Hippolyte déjà s'était plaint d'en souffrir; on n'y avait pris garde; il fallut reconnaître qu'il n'avait pas eu tort complètement, et on le laissa libre quelques heures. Mais à peine l'oedème eut-il un peu disparu, que les deux savants jugèrent à propos de rétablir le membre dans l'appareil, et en l'y serrant davantage, pour accélérer les choses.] (212)

But *what* is Charles trying to hasten? Flaubert again tries to throw us off the scent with his ironic reference to "the two men of science," another expression that is clearly intended to dismiss Charles as a fool. However, it is beyond doubt that a capable doctor (we know that he is not an "ass" despite what Doctor Canivet says) would be well aware that to *tighten* the grip on a limb in that condition could only hasten the onset of gangrene. Is it possible that Dr. Charles Bovary, who, like Gustave, was also the son of a doctor, did not know this? The hypothesis can reasonably be excluded. In the end Hippolyte's leg has to be amputated, and, paradoxically, this represents a victory for Charles, the moral masochist.[23]

Achille-Cléophas Flaubert, in the guise of Doctor Canivet, arrives from Neufchâtel and rapidly demotes Charles to the rank of *idiot de la famille*. It will be seen that this interweaving of the destinies of Bovary and Gustave Flaubert is not really arbitrary. Charles cannot consciously feel guilty, for this would lead to madness (as we shall see); nor can he accuse Emma or Homais, who had encouraged him, for this would create a precedent. Thus, Bovary decides that "fate must have had something to do with it [la fatalité s'en était mêlée]" (148/217).

This tendency to raise and then dash Emma's expectations, and the humiliation it causes, contributes to her slow destruction. What surprises her "is that she had ever thought that such a man could be worth anything, as if she had not already sufficiently observed his mediocrity at least twenty times! [c'était de s'être imaginé qu'un pareil homme pût valoir quelque chose, comme si vingt fois déjà elle n'avait pas suffisamment aperçu sa médiocrité!]" (149/218). Emma's reflection is relevant to this particular reading of the novel, for Flaubert seems here to sense and imply that Emma is not innocent but unconsciously in collusion with her husband.

Charles's behavior regularly conforms to set patterns: first he creates opportunities that deceive Emma into thinking that she can make amends for her unfaithfulness and for the humiliation she has caused him, and then he arouses disappointment and anger in her. When her anger is at its height, he then seizes the opportunity to be rejected. When Charles fails to cure the cripple, the situation develops as it had at the ball, when Emma had worn her saffron-colored dress:

> "Kiss me now, my love!"
> "Leave me alone," she said, pink with anger.
> "What's the matter now?" he kept saying, astounded. "Do calm down, you're not quite yourself! You know how I love you! Please!"
> "Stop it," she cried out with a terrible look. (150)

> ["Embrasse-moi donc, ma bonne!"
> "Laisse-moi," fit-elle, toute rouge de colère.
> "Qu'as-tu? qu'as-tu?" répétait-il stupéfait. "Calme-toi! reprendstoi! . . . Tu sais bien que je t'aime! . . . viens!"
> "Assez!" cria-t-elle d'un air terrible.] (219)

Charbovari's violence in this scene is chilling.

Rodolphe, then, becomes Emma's remedy against despair. Returning to him is a way of repressing her fury toward Charles, to whom she has continued to feel so attached that she has trusted in him despite all her previous frustrations. After Bovary's latest failure, however, the relationship between the two lovers suffers further deterioration: they make love no longer for pleasure but for the ephemeral satisfaction of soothing a growing sense of anguish. But when sex takes on this function, it becomes a drug, and the doses need to be increased:

Rodolphe sensed that in this love there lay further pleasures to be exploited. He reckoned all delicacy irksome. He used her brutishly. He made of her a creature docile and corrupt. Hers was a sort of idiot attachment, full of admiration for him, of pleasure for herself; a beatific drowsiness; and her soul sank deep into this fuddle, drowning there, shrivelling up, like the Duke of Clarence in his butt of malmsey. (154–55)

[Rodolphe aperçut en cet amour d'autres jouissances à exploiter. Il jugea toute pudeur incommode. Il la traita sans façon. Il en fit quelque chose de souple et de corrompu. C'était une sorte d'attachement idiot plein d'admiration pour lui, de voluptés pour elle, une béatitude qui l'engourdissait; et son âme s'enfonçait en cette ivresse et s'y noyait, ratatinée, comme le duc de Clarence dans son tonneau de malvoisie.] (224–25)

This deterioration of the relationship with her lover led one ingenuous critic (whose name escapes me) to assume that Emma had read the Marquis de Sade. Apart from the unacceptability of the hypothesis, the search for an external source of corruption such as the divine marquis surely implies denial of the ruinous nature of Emma's relationship with Charles. The reference to the Duke of Clarence would seem to suggest that in Flaubert's imagination Emma's punishment is already awaiting her: she will suffer death by drowning like Richard III's brother, but also like the mother of the child in the autobiographical nightmare described by Flaubert in *Mémoires d'un fou:* "I saw the water foaming and circles getting wider and wider until they disappeared [Je vis l'eau écumer, des cercles s'agrandir et disparaître]."[24] This nightmare will need further attention. Flaubert claims that it is Rodolphe who makes Emma both pliant and corrupt, but legend has it that it was the Duke of Clarence himself who, having been sentenced to death for high treason, chose the method of his execution. Can it be that the diabolical nature of Bovary's plan consists precisely in the fact that he makes his wife act as her own judge, torturer, and executioner while he plays the role of the victim?

At this point Emma assumes masculine characteristics and becomes increasingly phallic; she shows the traits of the prostitute, and like the prostitute she follows the pattern of being able to possess any man she wants, except one—the one who exploits her and is always out of reach.

Emma and old Madame Bovary were destined to clash. When they quarrel, Charles takes his mother's side and goes down on his knees to plead with his wife to desist. Emma senses the terrible threat implied in Charles's surrender to his mother and runs to Rodolphe for help: "'They're torturing me! I cannot bear it any more! Save me!' ['Ils sont à me torturer. Je n'y tiens plus! Sauve-moi!')" (156/226). However, the powerful bond that keeps Charles tied to his mother is double-edged, for it also fuels his destructive fury. In Bovary's unconscious fantasies only death can put an end to absolute dependence. And death, indeed, prepares to make its entrance.

Anxiety transforms Emma from a "jolie maîtresse" into the disturbed, avid, possessive woman from whom Rodolphe eventually flees. His letter of farewell is full of apparent hypocrisy, yet it also reveals his deepest fears: "Just like you, I didn't think about any of this at first, and I was slumbering in the shade of an ideal happiness, just like someone under the poison-tree, without heeding the consequences [Moi non plus, je n'y avais pas réfléchi d'abord, et je me reposais à l'ombre de ce bonheur idéal, comme à celle du mancenillier, sans prévoir les conséquences]" (164/236). Attention should be paid to the image of the "mancenillier," the poison-tree, which secretes such a highly toxic substance that anyone falling asleep under it is said to die. While Rodolphe presumably thinks he is just using a poetic image, Flaubert may be ironizing his character's need to flourish an erudite metaphor; in reality neither is aware of interpreting an unconscious fantasy. Emma, the maternal breast who surrendered herself on the grass—"she felt her heart, as it began to beat again, and the blood flowing in her body like a river of milk [elle sentait son coeur, dont les battements recommençaient, et le sang circuler dans sa chair comme un fleuve de lait]" (130/195)—becomes a breast producing a poisonous, sticky milk. These are anxieties of an almost psychotic nature, which originate in Charles but go on to contaminate Emma's relationship with her lover.[25]

Rodolphe's letter throws Emma into a state of despair. She had been partly responsible for this act of desertion through both her voracious desire for her lover and, at one stage, her lack of interest in him. If the present hypothesis is valid, then Rodolphe is quite unable to bear the oppressive pathology that surrounds him. When Emma is about to throw herself out of the window, it is Charles who saves her, who calls from afar, Charles who is "invisible and omnipotent, felt everywhere but not actually seen [invisible et tout-puissant, qu'on . . . sent partout, mais qu'on ne . . . voit pas]."[26] He seems never to lose touch for a single instant with that poor decaying heart; he forces her to eat, but "the food choked her [les morceaux l'étouffaient]" (166/239). If Charles not only unconsciously hates her but also loves her, we have similarly discovered that Emma also cares for Charles and is deeply attached to him. This is known to be a characteristic of all intensely sadomasochistic relationships. The pattern of their own latent relationship comes unmistakably to the surface during the subsequent episode in which Rodolphe's letter is mislaid.

Emma suddenly remembers the letter that proves they are lovers. Many readers will agree that losing that letter when the triangular relationship is so tense suggests the interference of a parapraxis.[27] The tiredness and *lassitude* she feels probably express an unconfessed wish not to get up. Remaining in the realm of hypothesis (which Flaubert repeatedly invites), Emma either wants Charles *to know* or hopes that a crisis will solve her difficulties, or perhaps she simply wishes to hurt Charles. Those who have found themselves in a similar plight know that such feelings can coexist. At one stage, Emma even asks Rodolphe whether he is carrying his pistols? Her astonished lover asks why: "'to defend yourself.' 'Against your husband? . . . I'd crush him with one finger' ['Pourquoi?' 'Mais . . . pour te défendre.' 'Est-ce de ton mari? Je l'écraserais d'une chiquenaude']" (136–37/203). Emma will not abandon her wishful image of Charles as a hero; she continues, so to speak, to invest in him.

Charles really has no need to read a letter. Emma herself fears that he knows everything—she is certain of it when he muses: "'It looks as if we won't be seeing Monsieur Rodolphe for a while' ['Nous ne sommes pas près, à ce qu'il paraît, de voir M. Ro-

dolphe']" (166/239). She catches her breath. Charles seems to be
going in for the kill:

"Why are you surprised? He goes off like that from time to time for a
change, and, I must say, I don't blame him. If a man has money and he's a
bachelor . . . In fact, he has a splendid time, does our friend. He's a real lad!
Monsieur Langlois was telling me." (167)

["Quoi donc t'étonne? Il s'absente ainsi de temps à autre pour se distraire, et,
ma foi, je l'approuve. Quand on a de la fortune et qu'on est garçon . . . Du
reste, il s'amuse joliment, notre ami! C'est un farceur. M. Langlois m'a
conté."] (239)

Note the necessarily refined timing of such maliciousness (this
time on the part of Flaubert, the scriptwriter of the sequence).

As Rodolphe's blue carriage crosses the village square at a brisk
trot, Emma lets out an anguished cry and falls to the ground. It is
as though Charles and Emma had decided to bring everything
out into the open. But this is not the end of the scene. As soon
as Emma regains consciousness, Charles is there yet again hover-
ing over her: "'Speak to me,' said Charles, 'speak to me! Come
on! It's me, your Charles who loves you! Don't you recognise
me? Look, here's your little girl, give her a hug!' ['Parle-nous!
Parle-nous! Remets-toi! C'est moi, ton Charles qui t'aime! Me
reconnais-tu? Tiens, voilà ta petite fille: embrasse-la donc!']"
(168/240). The child reaches out to her mother and wants to
embrace her, but Emma turns her head away and says with a
broken voice: "'No, no . . . nobody!' ['Non, non . . . personne!']"
(168/241). Then she faints again.

If it is true that Charles does unconsciously play cat and mouse
with Emma, then it is safe to assume that by so clumsily offering
himself and his daughter, the people whom Emma *ought* to love,
whose total devotion she *ought* to return, he is underlining all the
indignity and sordid baseness of which the woman is convinced
she is guilty. Charles seems bent on making her suffer the pangs
of guilt. When he tells her to take her daughter in her arms
(Charles is a doctor of his time and must have had experience of
women who fainted and the weakness they felt), such insistence,
just after having reminded her that Rodolphe is a womanizer and

will find a replacement in no time, reveals a strikingly vindictive vein of cruelty.

One feels like replying to Thibaudet that this is in fact the sort of psychological insight that brought innovation to the novel. Beneath the grayness of an impersonal style lies a Shakespearean throbbing of emotions—the kind of undistorted, uncompressed brutality that made Flaubert quiver: "if I were to see Shakespeare in person, I should die of fear! [Si je voyais Shakespeare en personne, je crèverais de peur!]."[28] Homais, whom Pio Baroja considered to be no more stupid than Flaubert—perhaps less— unconsciously evokes Shakespeare. It is not medicine that Emma needs: "'perhaps we ought to work on the imagination.' 'In what way? How do you mean?' said Bovary. 'Ah, that is the question. That is indeed the question: That is the question! as I read in the paper the other day.' ['il faudrait peut-être frapper l'imagination.' 'En quoi? Comment?' dit Bovary. 'Ah, c'est là la question! Telle est effectivement la question: *that is the question!* comme je lisais dernièrement dans le journal']" (169/242).

During Emma's illness, Charles is obsessed by feelings of guilt: "He reproached himself with forgetting about Emma; just as if, with his every thought belonging to this woman, it would have been swindling her out of something not to have her perpetually in mind [Il se reprochait d'en oublier Emma; comme si, toutes ses pensées appartenant à cette femme, c'eût été lui dérober quelque chose que de n'y pas continuellement réfléchir]" (171/245). This is pure remorse, caused by turning inward the aggressiveness he feels toward his wife as well as by the love he feels for her.[29] Nevertheless, as soon as Emma recovers, Charles compulsively repeats his former behavior. The grotesque episode at the theater, during the performance of *Lucia di Lammermoor,* should alone suffice to illustrate the fixed pattern of his unfathomable ambiguity.

Although the Bovarys are beginning to run short of money, Charles plays the gentleman and insists on taking Emma to the opera to celebrate her recovery; he spares no expense (especially as he is spending his mother's money!). At first Emma refuses on the grounds of her tiredness and the inconvenience and cost involved: "extraordinarily, Charles insisted, so convinced was he that the excursion must be beneficial for her [mais, par extraordinaire, Charles ne céda pas, tant il jugeait cette récréation lui devoir être profitable]" (178/253). The trap is being set:

Madame bought herself a hat, a pair of gloves, a bouquet. Monsieur worried dreadfully about missing the beginning; and, without even stopping to gulp down a plate of soup, they turned up at the theatre door, only to find it locked. (178)

[Madame s'acheta un chapeau, des gants, un bouquet. Monsieur craignait beaucoup de manquer le commencement; et, sans avoir eu le temps d'avaler un bouillon, ils se présentèrent devant les portes du théatre, qui étaient encore fermées.] (254)

Bovary's tension and apprehensive prudence are signs of an inner conflict. "Bovary prudently kept the tickets in his hand, in a trouser-pocket, pressed to his stomach [Bovary, par prudence, garda les billets à sa main, dans la poche de son pantalon, qu'il appuyait contre son ventre]" (179/255). Could Charles unconsciously be fighting his own wish to lose the tickets? He manages not to lose them, but he also repeatedly manages to irritate Emma.

He waits until his wife is rapt in the performance and then abruptly breaks in:

"But why," asked Bovary, "is that lord set on tormenting her?" "No, no," she replied, "that's her lover." "But he's swearing vengeance on her family, whereas the other one, the one that was on just now, said 'I love Lucia and I believe she loves me.' Anyway, he went off with her father, arm in arm. That is her father, isn't it, the ugly little one with the cock's feather in his hat?" (181)

["Pourquoi donc ce seigneur est-il à la persécuter?" "Mais non," réponditelle, "c'est son amant." "Pourtant il jure de se venger sur sa famille, tandis que l'autre, celui qui est venu tout à l'heure, disait 'J'aime Lucie et je m'en crois aimé.' D'ailleurs, il est parti avec son père, bras dessus, bras dessous. Car c'est bien son père, n'est-ce pas; le petit laid qui porte une plume de coq à son chapeau?"] (258)

In spite of his wife's explanations, Charles continues to misunderstand the plot:

He confessed, anyway, that he didn't understand the story—because of the music, which almost drowned out the words. "Does it matter?" said Emma. "Just be quiet!" "You know me," he said, leaning over her shoulder, "what I'm like, I need to be in the know." "Oh, do be quiet!" she said impatiently. (181)

[Il avouait, du reste, ne pas comprendre l'histoire—a cause de la musique—qui nuisait beaucoup aux paroles. "Qu'importe?" dit Emma; "Tais-toi!" "C'est que j'aime," reprit-il en se penchant sur son épaule, "a me rendre compte, tu sais bien." "Tais-toi! Tais-toi!" fit-elle, impatientée.] (258)

Charles is the petulant child who cannot understand adults and their complicated love affairs. It is at this point that he comes out with an amazing declaration: "I need to be in the know."

When he asks, "Why is that lord set on tormenting her?" it is as though he were asking, Why did you faint when Rodolphe's carriage went past? Emma is forced to suffer her husband's obtuseness. Homais offers ambiguous advice and considers Charles an idiot, while Rodolphe mocks him and thinks him comical and somewhat cowardly. To varying extents, everybody underestimates him. Yet Charles is left with the unavowed satisfaction of knowing that, after all, he is the cat and the others the mice. He is grotesquely maladroit and ends up ruining the performance he had made his wife so look forward to: he does not *understand* the explanations his wife offers him and continues to disturb her whenever the action requires intense concentration.

During the interval, the *maladroit* returns with a glass of barley water from the bar, where he has managed to spill three-quarters of a glass over the back of a woman from Rouen and been the object of insults and threats. He returns breathlessly with some news to tell Emma: "'You'll never guess who I bumped into up there! Monsieur Léon . . . The man himself! He's on his way over to pay his respects to you' ['Devine un peu qui j'ai rencontré là-haut? M. Léon . . . Lui-même! Il va venir te presenter ses civilités']" (183/260).

So far all of this can be ascribed to chance. Léon tries to find a way of seeing Emma again, probably to have the time to test the response of a woman with whom he had been so much in love. Bovary tells him that they are leaving the following day, but adds:

"'Unless . . . you would like to stay on alone, my pussy cat' ['A moins que tu ne veuilles rester seule, mon petit chat?']" (185/262), a gentle and extremely nonconformist term of endearment for a nineteenth-century country doctor to use. It is odd that no critic has called attention to Charles's extraordinary freedom from "provincial customs." Charles *insists* that Emma should stay on, and she stammers: "'The thing is . . . I'm not really . . . ' ['C'est que . . . je ne sais pas trop']." Charles continues: "'Well, think it over, we'll see how it looks in the morning' ['Eh bien, tu ré-fléchiras, nous verrons, la nuit porte conseil']" (185/263). The pattern of events resembles the episode when Emma went out riding with Rodolphe. Charles confirms his evident nonconformity and his wife goes on to commit adultery again.

If all these hypotheses are a key to understanding the context I have proposed, Flaubert appears to insist more vehemently on Bovary's restrained and disguised sadism and on his diabolical design (which are clearly shown to be rooted in his childhood) than on Emma's part in the complicity that she seems to find by and large acceptable. In this context, they are both victim and executioner at the same time: Charles always *misunderstands* Emma, but Emma seems unable to grasp Charles's need for love and tenderness—even less does she understand his sordid compulsion to wound her, to do her harm. She does not shore it up but gradually destroys him with a mass of lies and debts, and above all by killing herself.

Furthermore, as always happens in sadomasochistic relationships ever since the time of Shakespeare's Petruchio and Katherine, as happened between the first two Mesdames Bovary, who begin by deceiving each other but end up being allies and vying to torture poor Charles, Charles and Emma in a sense form an alliance and *use* other people—Hippolyte, Léon, Rodolphe, and even the innocent maid, Nastasie, whom Emma dismisses in a fit of anger and whom Charles does not defend. They form an alliance and use other people in pursuit of their slow but inexorable *jeu de massacre*.

Whenever she yields to her lovers, Emma never seems to forget her husband. After all, as soon as she has committed her first act of adultery with Rodolphe, what does she feel if not "the satisfaction of revenge [une satisfaction de vengeance]" (131/196) while they are out walking? The tragic game will continue to destroy Charles even after Emma has committed suicide.

Blindness

The relationship between Emma and Léon is no longer that of two adult lovers; it soon regresses and degenerates: "She used to call him child: 'Child, do you love me?' [Elle l'appelait enfant: 'Enfant, m'aimes-tu?']" (216/302). Emma acts "like a virtuous mother, . . . showing concern for his health and giving him advice in matters of conduct [comme une mère vertueuse . . . qui montrait des inquiétudes pour sa santé, lui donnait conseils sur sa conduite]," but then goes on to become a jealous, greedy, and possessive child obsessed with the fear of being abandoned. She wants to "strengthen her hold on him [le retenir davantage]" (230/318), keep him away from his friends, and even thinks about having him followed. Emma's behavior deteriorates and Léon begins to think that those who had wanted him to leave her might not have been wrong after all.[30]

On her way back home after one of her meetings with Léon, the adulteress reaches the top of a hill and hears a blind tramp singing:

Maids in the warmth of a summer day,
Dream of love, and of love always. (292 n)

Souvent la chaleur d'un beau jour
Fait rêver fillette à l'amour. (303)

The minor characters of the tramp and Homais's errand boy, Justin, who is desperately in love with Emma, seem suitable symbolic expressions of the two sides of Charles's ambivalent personality: the side of him that loves Emma to the point of idealization, as Flaubert loved Elise Schlésinger, might be represented by Justin, while the blind tramp might be seen to represent the sadistic side that wishes only to destroy, and definitively corrupts every effort to love. The tramp, moreover, will return with his song to deprive Emma of the chance to die in peace.

Love and hate are fused so inseparably that it is actually Justin, now "an excellent chambermaid [une excellente camériste]" (218/304), who provides Emma with the poison and does not warn anybody about it until it is too late. Indeed, so inseparably are such feelings fused that Gustave Flaubert once expressed the opinion that if a mother wanted to jump out of the window and her child opened it for her, this would be a great gesture of love: "I can think of nothing more tender [Je n'en sais pas de plus tendre]."[31]

The tramp is blind on two counts: because instead of eyelids he has "two yawning blood-stained holes [deux orbites béantes tout ensanglantées]," and because his face is concealed by "a squashed beaver-hat, bent down into the shape of a bowl [un vieux castor défoncé, s'arrondissant en cuvette]" (217/303): Oedipus concealed by Charbovari. The repulsive tramp's blindness might represent Charles as Oedipus, who, overwhelmed by guilt, gouges out his own eyes with Jocasta's brooch pins. The blindness caused by the old beaver hat seems almost to resemble the blindness of the talented masochist, which Charles adopts so that he can deny the sufferings of others and then continue to manipulate them. This recalls Charles's childhood hat, which was the symbol of his mother's exotic dreams rather than his (that hat combined the headgear of so many countries!). It could be taken as a symbol of the power of Charles's masochism, of the masochism with which Gustave, the idiot, the future *grand voyageur,* defied and provoked the derision of his schoolmates, proud in his sense of superiority—the sort of masochism that Charles is unable to see to the very end.

In his description of the tramp's voice as "a feeble wail at first," which then "became shrill [Sa voix, faible d'abord et vagissante, devenait aiguë]" (217/303), Flaubert almost seems to imply that what persecutes Emma has its origins in the early frustrations of the desperate infant.

Emma prevented Charles from seeing the end of *Lucia di*

Lammermoor by leaving the theater early; but the curtain now opens on the final tragic act of their life together. While Emma herself plays a part in her own destruction, as do other characters—Léon, Rodolphe, Lheureux—it is above all Charles who seems to hold the invisible strings. The circle closes and, at the same time, the themes become clear. Thanatos is born from the womb of *bêtise:* "Emma, crazed with sorrow, was shivering in her clothes, feeling her feet get colder and colder, sick at heart [Emma, ivre de tristesse, grelottait sous ses vêtements, et se sentait de plus en plus froid aux pieds, avec la mort dans l'âme]" (217/304).

Yet Charles is not blind at an unconscious level. He knows.[32] He knows about Léon, just as he had known about Rodolphe. The episode concerning Mademoiselle Lempereur, the piano teacher, provides further evidence that Charles knows about Emma's affair with Léon (after all, on the evening when his wife does not return from Yonville, does he not go directly to Léon's house, quite sure of finding her there?). This episode reveals the technique used by Charles to exploit his wife's feelings of guilt once he has caught her out. The piano lessons were the alibi that Emma had found as a cover for the secret meetings with her lover. Charles, however, does not bluntly say: "Mademoiselle Lempereur says she doesn't know you," as a simpleton might, but first asks: "'It's Mademoiselle Lempereur, isn't it, who gives you piano lessons?' ['C'est Mademoiselle Lempereur, n'est-ce pas, qui te donne des leçons?']." Only when Emma has fallen into the trap does he say: "'Well, I saw her just recently at Madame Liégeard's. I mentioned your name; and she's never heard of you.' It was like a thunderclap ['Eh bien, je l'ai vue tantôt chez Madame Liégeard. Je lui ai parlé de toi; elle ne te connaît pas.' Ce fut comme un coup de foudre]" (219/306). It is truly surprising that nobody, not even Sartre, seems to have noticed Bovary's strategy of demolition, not even when he now comes out into the open and intensifies his attack.

From this moment on, Emma's life is nothing but "a tissue of lies [un assemblage de mensonges]" (220/307). It is just a bartering process involving promissory notes, subterfuge, and growing despair: "A panorama of attainable fantasies now unfolded before Emma's eyes [Un horizon de fantaisies réalisables s'ouvrit alors devant Emma]" (222/309). This is her final attempt to avoid total breakdown. Charles has granted Emma general power of attorney in a document drawn up by Léon, who is a deputy notary public. This surrender is the means by which Charles achieves his final sadistic victory.[33] Everything is arranged to make Emma feel increasingly abject.

When Charles's mother interferes again, he skillfully manages to play one woman off against the other, succeeding in humiliating and upsetting both of them. Bovary's mother senses what is happening and demands that her daughter-in-law renounce the power of attorney, which indeed ends up in the fire: "Emma began to laugh, a loud strident continuous laugh: she was having a nervous attack [Emma se mit à rire d'un rire strident, éclatant, continu: elle avait une attaque de nerfs]" (223/311). But this time not even his mother is spared: "'Oh, my God!' shouted Charles. 'It's just as much your fault! Coming here, making a scene with her!' ['Ah! mon Dieu! s'écria Charles. 'Eh! tu as tort aussi, toi! Tu viens lui faire des scènes!']." For the first time, just when his mother is in the right for once, he rebels and takes his wife's side, choosing the time and manner so well that his mother leaves the house: "'You love her more than you love me, and quite right too, that's just as it should be. Anyway, so be it. You'll see' ['Tu l'aimes mieux que moi, et tu as raison, c'est dans l'ordre. Au reste, tant pis! Tu verras!']" (224/311).

Now that it is too late, now that the process of deterioration is irreversible, Charles not only sacrifices his belongings to Emma by signing another power of attorney but also sacrifices his mother to her. He can no longer be accused of anything! Thus, Emma's despair sinks to its greatest depths:

What exuberance, the following Thursday, at the hotel, in their room, with Léon. She laughed, she cried, she sang, she danced, she sent down for ices, she wanted to smoke cigarettes; and he thought her extravagant, but adorable, superb. He had no idea what reaction of her entire being it was, driving her harder to throw herself into the pleasures of the flesh. She was becoming irritable, greedy and voluptuous. She walked through the streets with him, unabashed, oblivious, she said, of compromising herself. (224)

[Quel débordement, le jeudi d'après, à l'hôtel, dans leur chambre, avec Léon! Elle rit, pleura, chanta, dansa, fit monter des sorbets, voulut fumer des cigarettes, lui parut extravagante, mais adorable, superbe. Il ne savait pas quelle réaction de tout son être la poussait davantage à se précipiter sur les jouissances de la vie. Elle devenait irritable, gourmande, et voluptueuse; et elle se promenait avec lui dans les rues, tête haute, sans peur, disait-elle, de se compromettre.] (311)

Even the relationship between Emma and Léon seems to be reshaped by forces that no longer obey common rules. All that is left to Léon is to play a passive, feminine role in the face of these new, dark, and implacable laws:

He became her mistress rather than she becoming his. She spoke tender words mingled with kisses that carried his soul away. Where could she have learned such corruption, almost intangible, so profoundly had it been dissembled? (226)

[Il devenait sa maîtresse plutôt qu'elle n'était la sienne. Elle avait des paroles tendres avec des baisers qui lui emportaient l'âme. Où donc avait-elle appris cette corruption, presque immatérielle à force d'être profonde et dissimulée?] (313)

The idealizations that Emma has created so as not to give in to despair begin to crumble: "Never touch your idols: the gilding will stick to your fingers [Il ne faut pas toucher aux idoles: la dorure en reste aux mains]" (229/317). Death and coldness come between the two lovers, who often find themselves talking about things that have nothing to do with their love. After each period of separation,

Emma came back to him more inflamed, more voracious. Her undressing was brutal, tearing at the delicate laces on her corset, which rustled down over her hips, like a slithering snake. She tiptoed over on bare feet to check once again that the door was locked, and in one motion she shed all her clothes; pale and silent and serious, she fell upon him, shivering. (229–30)

[Emma revenait à lui plus enflammée, plus avide. Elle se déshabillait bru-talement, arrachant le lacé mince de son corset, qui sifflait autour de ses hanches comme une couleuvre qui glisse. Elle allait sur la pointe des ses pieds nus regarder encore une fois si la porte était fermée, puis elle faisait d'un seul geste tomber ensemble tous ses vêtements; et pâle, sans parler, sérieuse, elle s'abattait contre sa poitrine, avec un long frisson.] (318)

She checks the door obsessively. Might this action ultimately express her wish for Charles to break in?

Every effort to revive their love is made in vain: "'And yet I love him,'" she told herself . . . No matter! She was not happy, had never been so. Where did it come from, this feeling of depriva-tion, this instantaneous decay of the things in which she put her trust? ['Je l'aime pourtant,' se disait-elle . . . N'importe! Elle n'était pas heureuse, ne l'avait jamais été. D'où venait donc cette insuffisance de la vie, cette pourriture instantanée des choses où elle s'appuyait?]" (231/319). It is Eros making one last attempt to rebel, accepting the compromises of neurosis but rejecting madness.

The specters of oral sadism haunting Flaubert's imagery multi-ply: the devourer of Bovary's inheritance, Lheureux-Vinçart, who "was bleeding himself white [se saignait]" for Emma, is seen as "a sly dog and a shark [mâtin et tigre]" (246/337); Emma bargains "rapaciously [avec rapacité]" (247/338); she thinks of Léon and would give anything to have one more of those secret meetings "which sated her [qui la rassasiaent]" (235/324). The blind man rolls his greenish eyes, shows his tongue, and rubs his hands on his belly, letting out "a kind of muffled howl, like a ravenous dog [une sorte de hurlement sourd, comme un chien affamé]" (244/335). Despite the bad state of her teeth, Madame Homais devours chocolate confectioneries bought by her hus-band in rue Massacre. The pharmacist prescribes diets "while eating his cutlet and drinking his tea [mangeant sa côtelette et buvant son thé]" (246/337), the notary covers Emma's hand "with a greedy kiss [d'un baiser vorace]" (247/337). Madame Roulet, the nurse, briefly seems to offer the only refuge.

Charles strips himself of all his possessions and is even ruining his ultimate resource, his profession, while his wife can no longer control her anguish: "Terror-stricken, she would scream. Charles would come rushing in. 'Oh, do go away!' she would say [Souvent une terreur la prenait, elle poussait un cri, Charles accourait. 'Ah! va-t-en!' disait-elle]" (235/324).

The circle closes as Emma is transformed into the phantom that has haunted Charles since childhood: "the vague pernicious creature, the siren, the fantastical monster that lives down in the fathomless places of love [la vague créature pernicieuse, la sirène, le monstre, qui habite fantastiquement les profondeurs de l'amour]," the very specter that defeated all of Gustave Flaubert's desperate attempts to love. In this, he was like Léon, a man of the pandects with "his head full of harems [avec les harems dans la tête]," for "every bourgeois, in the heat of youth, if only for a day, if only for a minute, has believed himself capable of immense passions, of heroic enterprises. The most mediocre libertine has dreamed of oriental princesses; every notary carries about inside him the debris of a poet [Tout bourgeois, dans l'échauffement de sa jeunesse, ne fût-ce qu'un jour, une minute, s'est cru capable d'immenses passions, de hautes enterprises. Le plus médiocre libertin a rêvé des sultanes; chaque notaire porte en soi les débris d'un poète]" (236/325).

Emma is smitten with remorse, with an immense regret that kindles her anxiety rather than soothing it, while Charles just sits poking the fire "placidly, with his feet on the fender [avec placidité, les deux pieds sur les chenets]" (241/331). What bitterness and regret she feels—but Charles's kindness and understanding might yet offer salvation! Having sought every possible solution, she now imagines telling him everything:

"Keep off! This carpet under your feet is no longer ours. Not a chair, not a pin, not a feather in your own house, and it's me, I'm the one who has ruined you, poor man!" There would be a great sob, and he would weep copiously, and eventually, once over the shock, he would forgive. (248)

["Retire-toi. Ce tapis où tu marches n'est plus à nous. De ta maison, tu n'as pas un meuble, une épingle, une paille, et c'est moi qui t'ai ruiné, pauvre homme!" Alors ce serait un grand sanglot, puis il pleurerait abondamment, et enfin, la surprise passée, il pardonnerait]. (339)

But when Charles's goodness is needed it turns out to be a barren hope:

"Yes," she muttered as she ground her teeth, "he will forgive me, the man I could never pardon for just knowing me even if he had a million . . . Never! Never!" This idea of Bovary's superiority was exasperating to her. (248)

["Oui," murmurait-elle en grinçant les dents, "il me pardonnera, lui qui n'aurait pas assez d'un million à m'offrir pour que je l'excuse de m'avoir connue . . . Jamais! jamais!" Cette idée de la supériorité de Bovary sur elle l'exaspérait.] (339)

Emma implores everybody except her good husband, Charles. All that is left to her is delirium.

She senses the threat that her husband represents and goes to see Mère Rolet: "she had rushed over, pursued by a sort of panic that thrust her out of her own home [elle y était accourue, poussée par une sorte d'épouvante qui la chassait de sa maison]" (250/341). After one final visit to Rodolphe, madness overcomes her. Justin indicates the way out by showing her where the powder that will poison her is kept.

A Matter of Fate

The love between Emma and Charles becomes fully evident only when all is lost. When Charles realizes that Emma has taken poison, that he will lose her forever, he is at last able to look at her with infinite tenderness, "with a tenderness in his eyes that she had never seen before [une tendresse comme elle n'en avait jamais vu]." "'Don't cry!' she said. 'Soon, I shan't torment you ever again!' And she ran her fingers through his hair, slowly ['Ne pleure pas!' lui dit-elle. 'Bientôt je ne te tourmenterai plus!' Et elle lui passait la main dans les cheveux, lentement]." Charles senses the spontaneity of her gesture and is overwhelmed by despair—just when Emma shows him "such a love as she had never shown to him before [plus d'amour que jamais]" (259/350). He does everything in his power to save her, and even calls in Larivière, the eminent physician.

While the doctor and the Homais family are eating at the final banquet, Charles and Emma remain alone to await death. While the priest gives absolution, he passes judgment:

The priest . . . dipped his right thumb in the oil, and began the unctions: first upon the eyes, which had so coveted worldly splendours; then upon her nostrils, so greedy for warm breezes and amorous perfumes; then upon the mouth, which had uttered lying words, which had groaned with pride and cried out in lustfulness. (265)

[Le prêtre trempa son pouce droit dans l'huile et commença les onctions: d'abord sur les yeux, qui avaient tant convoité toutes les somptuosités terrestres; puis sur les narines, friandes de brises tièdes et de senteurs amoureuses; puis sur la bouche, qui s'était ouverte pour le mensonge, qui avait gémi d'orgueil et crié dans la luxure.] (357)

The moralism of society would bury everything under the blanket term "bovarysme":

The priest arose and took the crucifix; now she stretched forth her neck like one in thirst, and, pressing her lips to the body of the Man-God, she laid upon him with all her ebbing strength the greatest loving kiss she had ever given. (265)

[Le prêtre se releva pour prendre le crucifix; alors elle allongea le cou comme quelqu'un qui a soif, et, collant ses lèvres sur le corps de l'Homme-Dieu, elle y déposa de toute sa force expirante le plus grand baiser d'amour qu'elle eût jamais donné.] (357)

To Emma, Charles is Christ the persecutor and persecuted, a figure who has crucified her by turning the other cheek and taking upon himself all the sins, but who is already beginning to die. One cannot help but recall Auerbach's momentary blindness when he wrote that nobody would ever want to call *Madame Bovary* a story about love.[34]

When Emma dies, Charles locks himself in his study, picks up his pen, sobs for a few minutes, and then writes:

I wish her to be buried in her wedding dress, with white shoes and a crown of flowers. Her hair is to be arranged loosely about her shoulders: three coffins, one of oak, one of mahogany, one of lead. Let no one speak to me

47

and I shall manage. Cover everything over with a large piece of green velvet. Such is my wish. Let it be done. (268)

[Je veux qu'on l'enterre dans sa robe de noces, avec des souliers blancs, une couronne. On lui étalera les cheveux sur les épaules; trois cercueils, un de chêne, un d'acajou, un de plomb. Qu'on ne me dise rien, j'aurai de la force. On lui mettra pardessus tout une grande pièce de velour vert. Je le veux. Faites-le.] (361)

For his fellow townsmen, these are just romantic notions. Charles loses his temper and demands that his wishes be obeyed. The episode has all the appearance of being a manic attempt to hold back his own tears: the whole letter, with its final words, "Such is my wish. Let it be done," is a royal command. For once in his life, between one death and the next, Charles becomes both King in Thebes and Prince in Mycenae in an attempt to shore up "the immensity of his sadness [l'immensité de son chagrin]" (280/375).

A sadomasochistic relationship might be compared to a war in which feelings of guilt are strangely reciprocal: while the war lasts the ordeal is suspended. Until divine decree points to the guilty party, each partner can blame the other for his or her unhappiness, either consciously, as Emma does, or unconsciously, as is probably the case with Charles. With the death of Emma—who, in taking her own life, above all takes revenge—the pact is broken and the terrible divine response is unleashed. Thus, even the old armor that Charles used to deny recognition of Emma's suffering now falls apart, leaving him to face up to the fact that he has destroyed the woman he loved.

Charles's peremptory instructions contain all of the themes that run through the tragedy: the immaculate virgin who had married in white, the crowned queen, and the many regal women who obsessed Gustave-Charles—from the faithless Isabel of Bavaria to Marguerite of Burgundy, the incestuous queen bee of the bloody orgies in the Tower of Nesle. "Her hair is to be arranged loosely about her shoulders" so that she may resemble the repentant Mary Magdalene, and then she is to be enclosed in three coffins. For the first time Charles rebels even against God, crying blasphemously: "I hate that God of yours! [Je l'exècre, votre Dieu!]" (269/362).

It was suggested earlier that, by playing the role of the innocent victim, Charles ensnares Emma so as to be able to crush her under the weight of guilt. Once the tragedy is consummated, his fantasies seem to lend credence to this idea, especially when he sees Emma covered with a fine cobweb, and he feels "that an infinite mass, an enormous weight, lay pressing upon her [que des masses infinies, qu'un poids énorme pesait sur elle]" (270/363). Yet he, too, will be crushed by the weight of guilt.

Charles does not know how to deal with his terrible sense of guilt and is not even able to realize that it is *he* who has woven the web of his own nightmare. The only way he can fight his torment is with another omnipotent fantasy: "he told himself that by wishing it with all his might, he could perhaps bring her back to life [il se disait qu'en le voulant extrèmement, il parviendrait peut-être à la ressusciter]" (270/364). He is unable to admit consciously to himself that although he has loved Emma to distraction, he has also hated and feared her, and so he must continue denying everything. Does he perhaps wish to have her enclosed in three coffins to prevent her ghost from returning to haunt him? And yet Emma does come back to corrupt him "from beyond the grave [par-delà le tombeau]" (280/376) by compelling him to adopt her tastes and ideas. He buys himself patent leather shoes, wears white ties, waxes his moustache, and, like her, starts signing promissory notes. In order to protect himself from this ghost, he adopts a primitive mechanism that psychoanalysts call identification with the aggressor.

Charles then finds the first piece of evidence, Rodolphe's letter of farewell: "a little R at the bottom of the second page. What did it mean? He remembered Rodolphe's little attentions, his sudden disappearance and the awkwardness in his manner when they had met since then, two or three times [un petit R au bas de la seconde page. Qu'était-ce? Il se rappela les assiduités de Rodolphe, sa disparition soudaine et l'air contraint qu'il avait eu en le rencontrant depuis, deux ou trois fois]." But even then he finds a means of explaining it away: "'Perhaps they loved one another platonically,' he said to himself ['Ils se sont peut-être aimés platoniquement,' se dit-il]." So nothing had escaped his attention after all! Now that he has the evidence before his very eyes, the images return, and with them the need for self-deception: "he shied away from the evidence, and his faltering jealousy was lost in the immensity of his sadness [il recula devant les preuves, et sa jalousie incertaine se perdit dans l'immensité de son chagrin]" (280/375).

This would have been quite sufficient proof that Charles is no imbecile. An imbecile has no need to reject or deny so vehemently—an imbecile simply does not understand or make mental connections.

Flaubert, moreover, handles the whole of the letter episode with impressive mastery, perfectly orchestrating the reactions of the characters so that the reader becomes involved to the extent of believing that Bovary has already seen it. His final reaction (it had been only platonic love!) is meant to cause us yet another disappointment. As far as Charles is concerned nobody is guilty, just as no one had been responsible for the amputation of Hippolyte's leg. What had been "a curse" when he was talking to Père Rouault becomes purely "a matter of fate" when he talks to Rodolphe. Charles even denies being involved as a victim. It is all to be blamed on fate and nobody has the power to fight against fate—the fate that Charles himself actually administers in some dark corner of his soul.

However, it will be seen that omnipotence is the refuge of the helpless child in the face of insurmountable hostile forces. Throughout his life Charles has had to struggle against the specter of a burdensome mother "who had shifted onto this childish head all her scattered and broken vanities [qui reporta sur cette tête d'enfant toutes ses vanités éparses, brisées]" (5/39):

It was peculiar, that Bovary, though he thought continually of Emma, began to forget her face; and he was in despair as he felt the image slipping from his memory no matter what he did to keep hold of it. (283)

[Une chose étrange, c'est que Bovary, tout en pensant à Emma continuellement, l'oubliait; et il se désespérait à sentir cette image lui échapper de la mémoire au milieu des efforts qu'il faisait pour la retenir.] (378)

He appears to want to hold on to the memory of the woman he loves and, at the same time, be rid of the ghost that haunts him. Every night he has the same dream: he approaches Emma, but when he is about to embrace her, she rots away in his arms. Is Emma really the woman he sees in his dream? Charles believes she is.

The inability to forget her or to reconstruct her in his mind lacerates him to the extent that all his defenses break down:

Out of respect, or out of a sort of sensuality that made him wish to linger in his investigations, Charles had not yet opened up the secret compartment in the rosewood desk that Emma had generally used. One day, at last, he sat down, turned the key and pushed the spring. All the letters from Léon were there. No doubt about it, this time! He devoured them right down to the last line, rummaged about in every corner, in every piece of furniture, in every drawer, along the walls, sobbing and roaring, out of his mind. He discovered a box, smashed it open with a kick. Staring him straight in the face was the portrait of Rodolphe, in among a toppling pile of love letters. (284)

[Par respect, ou par une sorte de sensualité qui lui faisait mettre de la lenteur dans ses investigations, Charles n'avait pas encore ouvert le compartiment secret d'un bureau de palissandre dont Emma se servait habituellement. Un jour, enfin, il s'assit devant, tourna la clef et poussa le ressort. Toutes les lettres de Léon s'y trouvaient. Plus de doute, cette fois! Il dévora jusqu'à la dernière, fouilla dans tous les coins, tous les meubles, tous les tiroirs, derrière les murs, sanglotant, hurlant, éperdu, fou. Il découvrit une boîte, la défonça d'un coup de pied. Le portrait de Rodolphe lui sauta en plein visage, aux milieu des billets doux bouleversés.] (380)

In a letter dated 1852, Gustave wrote to Louise Colet: "There comes a time when one needs to hurt oneself, to hate one's flesh, to throw mud in one's face, so hideous does that flesh seem [Il arrive un moment où l'on a besoin de se faire souffrir, haïr sa chair, de lui jeter de la boue au visage, tant elle vous semble hideuse]."[35] For the first and last time in his life Charles lifts the hat that has been covering his eyes. Moved by remorse and a sort of deconsecrating sensuality, Bovary renounces his "blindness." He abandons the *respect* that had allowed him to continue considering Emma a superior woman and rejects the idealization that had helped him to put order into his passions.

With skillful restraint, Flaubert brings to the surface all of the voluptuousness underlying Charles's search for clues, his morbid hesitation to acknowledge what he already knows unconsciously. *Sensualité* and *lenteur* seem to permeate his subsequent actions: "One day, at last, he sat down, turned the key and pushed the spring [Un jour, enfin, il s'assit devant, tourna la clef et poussa le ressort]." The scene evokes the excitement of the seasoned gambler as he slowly fans out his cards and discovers the hand he has been dealt, the emotion of the delinquent who performs forbidden acts, of the child who stands outside his parents' bedroom door. Suspense and the need to delay the game, which have perspicaciously been identified as characteristics of masochism, are also present in the culminating moments of Bovary's tragedy.[36] In reality, he opens the little rosewood chest when he really wants to; it is he who chooses the moment to learn that he has always been involved in a three-way relationship.

Charles becomes a pathetic figure:

He never went out, had no visitors, even refused to go and see his patients. It was said he'd shut himself away with the bottle. Sometimes, though, the curious would hoist themselves up onto the garden hedge, and observe in amazement a wild man with a long beard, dressed in shabby clothes, weeping out loud as he went along. (284–85)

[Il ne sortait plus, ne recevait personne, refusait même d'aller voir ses malades. Alors on prétendit qu'il s'enfermait pour boire. Quelquefois pourtant, un curieux se haussait pardessus la haie du jardin, et apercevait avec ébahissement cet homme à barbe longue, couvert d'habits sordides, farouche, et qui pleurait tout haut en marchant.] (380)

The idea that some inquisitive passerby might look through the window and see him in such a state of despair reflects another of Charles's secret aspirations. Flaubert immediately confirms this: "But his voluptuous sorrow was incomplete, for he had no one there to share it with him [La volupté de sa douleur était incomplète, car il n'avait autour de lui personne qui la partageât]" (285/380).

The defeat of a masochist is meaningless if it cannot be exhibited and subtly reproved. The harmless spectator to whom Charles chooses to pour out all his sorrows is the innkeeper, Mère Lefrançois. A mother. Might this be the return of old Madame Bovary, the figure whose cloying expectations had made Charles grow up to be such a disappointing man? The dream that haunts the widower, as we have seen, represents his dramatic ambivalence: "always it was the same dream: he came nearer; but when he went to embrace her, she turned to putrid flesh in his arms [c'était toujours le même rêve: il s'approchait d'elle; mais, quand il venait à l'étreindre, elle tombait en pourriture dans ses bras]" (283/378). Where does that sense of decomposition and death come from if not from deep within Charles? The hatred he felt for his mother, which had been repressed and transformed into total devotion, returns to dissolve the desperate strength of his love. If this assumption is plausible, then Charles's outpourings when he is with Mère Lefrançois correspond to the accusation implicit in the confusion of transference: just look at what you have done to me!

But that very *pourriture*, that sense of putrefaction, enables us to associate Charles's despair with the insufficiency of life and the instantaneous putrefaction of the things on which she leaned felt by Père Rouault's daughter, the future Madame Bovary. Just how much of this despair did Emma manage to transmit to her husband?

When Charles and Rodolphe Boulanger meet for the last time, they both turn pale but then go off to have a beer together. Rodolphe talks and chews on his cigar but Charles isn't listening, for he is lost in reverie as he looks at the face that Emma had loved: "he so wanted to have been this other man [il aurait voulu être cet homme]" (285/381). The encounter brings out Bovary's unfulfilled homosexual desires, the attraction to that phallic power that he does not possess and that he would probably gladly appropriate in order to be able to face up to the woman he both loves and fears (he had earlier prostrated himself before the Viscount's cigars). Charles seems to be sensually attracted by the face across the table from him, a face that gradually grows redder while the nostrils flare and the lips tremble . . . And at last a flash of hatred glimmers in his eyes. Hatred, because those desires comprise long-standing resentment toward the charming assistant army surgeon who had abandoned his paternal role: "there was even a moment when Charles, brimming with a sombre fury, fixed his eyes on Rodolphe, who, in some terror, stopped talking [il y eut même un instant où Charles, plein d'une fureur sombre, fixa ses yeux contre Rodolphe, qui, dans une sorte d'effroi, s'interrompit]" (285/381). But it is only passing fury, for Charles, who has spent his life feeling barely tolerated, cannot allow himself the slightest aggressiveness: "'I don't hold it against you,' he said ['Je ne vous en veux pas,' dit-il]," and concludes that "'fate is to blame' ['C'est la faute de la fatalité!']" (286/381). Rodolphe, who believed that he alone had guided the hand of fate, finds Bovary somewhat comical and a little cowardly!

After the death of Charles an autopsy is conducted, but "nothing was found [on ne trouva rien!]" (286/382). Flaubert seems to want to disprove every one of our hypotheses: inside Bovary there is nothing but the emptiness of imbecility. It is we who have imagined everything: "my secret intention," wrote Flaubert, "is to confuse the reader to such a point that he is driven mad [c'est mon but secret: ahurir tellement le lecteur qu'il en devienne fou]."[37]

A Wholly Fictitious Story

It would perhaps be useful at this stage to take a closer look at both the historical and the psychological correspondences between Gustave Flaubert and Charles Bovary. Although this consideration will not be even minimally beneficial to a reading of the novel, it will offer another chance to glimpse the miracle of literary creation. Insistence upon the relationship between the author and his pathology would be meaningless if it did not allow us to contemplate with admiration the mysterious ability of genius to rise above all too human limitations.[38]

It is difficult not to agree with Unamuno's comments about the supposed impersonality and invisibility of Flaubert the author: "The whole man is there in his work, this man who is said to be absent and himself declared that he did not appear in his own works. In fact this is not true and never could be."[39] When Flaubert assures Madame Chatepie that "[t]here is nothing real in *Madame Bovary*. It is a wholly fictitious story; it contains nothing regarding either my feelings or my life [*Madame Bovary* n'a rien de vrai. C'est une histoire totalement inventée; je n'y ai rien mis de mes sentiments ni de mon existence],"[40] he is making a statement that no writer would subscribe to after Freud.

Was Flaubert cheating or did he really believe what he said? His *Mémoires d'un fou* and *Passion et vertu* bear an epigraph taken from Shakespeare's *Romeo and Juliet:* "Thou canst not speak of that thou dost not feel." The second volume of Flaubert's *Oeuvres complètes,* published by Editions du Seuil, has as an epigraph an intuitive remark taken from the *Correspondance:* "One doesn't choose a subject. This is something that neither readers nor critics understand. The secret of a masterpiece lies in the agreement of the subject matter with the author's temperament [On ne choisit pas son sujet. Voilà ce que le public et les critiques ne comprennent pas. Le secret des chefs-d'oeuvre est là, dans la concordance du sujet et du tempérament de l'auteur]."

All of us accept certain images of ourselves and reject others. It was essentially while he was discovering the mechanisms of this rejection that Freud constructed his theory of the unconscious. Heinrich Heine refused to believe in the theft of which Rousseau accused himself in the *Confessions*—for which an innocent housemaid is supposed to have been dismissed.[41] And Edmund Bergler, unlike the more naïve Geneviève Mouillaud,[42] does not believe Stendhal's autobiographical confession of his Oedipal love for his mother: this incestuous desire of the child, so clearly perceived and confessed after a few decades have elapsed, is embarrassing simply because other mortals, who just as typically go through the

Oedipal phase, repress the experience.[43] What Rousseau, Stendhal, and Flaubert (in his statement "Madame Bovary c'est moi") affirm is only what they are consciously prepared to admit as being true of themselves and are willing to communicate to the reader. In other words, they confess the lesser sin in order to deny the greater one.

The direction this discussion is taking may well find firm opposition in some quarters, beginning with Marcel Proust: Francesco Orlando, for example, has fought against and theorized about both the risks and the arbitrariness involved in shifting from the psychoanalysis of characters to that of their authors. I shall therefore attempt to confute a few stereotyped statements, such as those of Enid Starkie, who has written that Charles, being "a slow-witted, uncouth bourgeois, in the modern sense of the word, and also devoid of both sensitivity and imagination,"[44] represents everything that Flaubert most abhorred.

However, let me say straightaway that I am *not* suggesting that Charbovari corresponds to the "real Flaubert" or his deepest self. I simply wish to point out that the character Charles has more than one surprising trait in common with Gustave. These are perhaps the characteristics least cherished by Flaubert and therefore those which are most intensely repressed or split off. But this may be the very reason why he invests them with such overwhelming dramatic potential.[45]

At the beginning and at the end of the novel, there are two extremely brief allusions that deserve attention. The indications are too slight to allow bold assertions, yet they do permit investigation in two directions that are quite different from those implied in Flaubert's admission "Madame Bovary c'est moi."

Despite the similarity of their destinies, Bovary has more in common with Gustave Flaubert than with Eugène Delamaro, as Maxime du Camp and Louis Bouilhet proposed. Similarly, Emma has more in common with Gustave, his mother, and his sister than with Delphine Couturier, or Louise Pradier (as some critics believe), or Louise Colet, as she herself thought.[46] This is what I should like to demonstrate.

The first chapter begins with the now famous words: "We were at Prep, when the Head came in, followed by a new boy not in uniform [Nous étions à l'étude, quant le Proviseur entra, suivi d'un nouveau, habillé en bourgeois]" (1/35). Flaubert uses *nous* seven times in the first chapter, which tells us that he was there and knew Charles well. After this initial appearance, at least in the definitive edition of the work, the author withdraws to the heights of his Olympus.

Why does he give us this information? How does this use of *nous* affect the economy of the novel? Obsessive as he was, he must have given it great thought. Traditional criticism might answer that *nous* is a figure that leads back to the narrator. My proposal is that this could at most be the *conscious* answer. However, we have agreed to attribute only relative importance to all that is conscious or commonsensical.

We were earlier wondering why Flaubert insists quite so much on Charles's upbringing. One hypothesis might be that Flaubert unconsciously wishes to warn us that his knowledge of both facts and characters derives from a sort of fellowship with Charles Bovary. The most plausible supposition (which does not exclude the others but underpins them) is that Flaubert here splits himself in two, as can happen to any of us in dreams, in an attempt to censure what he does not wish to accept, that Gustave-the-schoolboy sees in Charles-the-new-boy the sadistic and masochistic part of himself. Furthermore, we know that this would not be the first such split: Gustave Antouskothi Koclott and the Garçon are only two of many instances of splitting (quite probably more conscious) that have been readily accepted by the majority of critics.

That *nous*, however, is undoubtedly thought provoking. Is this technical expedient "curious," as Jean Rousset calls it,[47] or is it "puzzling," as Victor Brombert says?[48] Or might it be one of those subtle compromises with which Flaubert's art of modulation guides us to the very heart of the tragedy, while fully exploiting ironic detachment and the possibilities it offers? This is difficult to deny. But it is possible to ascribe meaning even to *the choice* of expedient, just as one can to the choice of a word, sequence, metaphor, or metonymy.

Having shown very little interest during the whole novel in Berthe—the daughter of Emma and Charles—Flaubert makes a brief reference to her future once her parents are dead and the novel is nearing its end:

> Once everything had been sold, there were just twelve francs and seventy-five cents left over, which was enough to pay for Mademoiselle Bovary's journey to her grandmother's house. The good lady died that same year; because Père Rouault was paralysed, it was an aunt who took her in. She is poor and she sends the girl to earn her living in a cotton-mill. (286)

> [Quand tout fut vendu, il resta douze francs soixante et quinze centimes qui servirent à payer le voyage de Mlle Bovary chez sa grand-mère. La bonne femme mourut dans l'année même: le père Rouault étant paralysé, ce fut une tante qui s'en chargea. Elle est pauvre et l'envoie, pour gagner sa vie, dans une filature de coton.] (381)

With only slight variations, young Mademoiselle Bovary faces the same series of vicissitudes as those suffered by Caroline Fleuriot, Gustave's mother. She had also been passed round from one relative to another—hence Sartre's comment: "they would rather die than take care of her."[49] Caroline and Berthe, then, were both unwanted children. To continue the comparison with dream subjects, a classical psychoanalyst might have added that the reversal of family relationships (the daughter instead of the mother, the son instead of the father, and so forth) is yet another distorting artifice by means of which a relationship that one wishes to censure is made accessible to the conscious mind. Pursuing this direction of thought (to which I am ascribing only relative value), I could add that in an early work by Flaubert, *Rage et impuissance* (rage and impotence, two components of Charles's personality), Berthe happens to be the name of an elderly servant.[50]

Through these allusions, Flaubert makes a connection between himself and Charles and evokes the figure of his mother, thus appearing to say that *Madame Bovary* is a story about his family.

Les Imbéciles!

Flaubert offers further correlations between Charles Bovary and himself. Both were sons of surgeons who had been ill-disposed toward the arts; Gustave, like Charles, had been a quiet little boy, as Caroline de Commanville recalls in her *Souvenirs intimes*.[51] Charles was naïve, just as Gustave was judged to be by many people—from Léon Daudet, who christened him the "grand naïf,"[52] to P. M. Wetherill, who completes his description with the words of Maxime du Camp: "He was gullible and easily deceived quite simply because he never told lies and was incapable of imagining that anybody might want to deceive him."[53]

Again like Charles, Gustave suffered a setback during his studies (he failed his law exam), and both shared the unfortunate distinction of being laughed at by teachers and schoolmates alike. And this is surely quite a significant similarity. *Mémoires d'un fou*, which is considered to be openly autobiographical, contains the following passage:

Imbeciles! And *they* laughed at *me!* They who were so weak, so common, so narrow-minded; at me, a mind that was drowning on the far edges of creation, lost in the worlds of poetry. I felt greater than all of them; my satisfaction was immense and I experienced such heavenly ecstasy before the intimate revelations of my soul! I felt as great as the world itself: and yet if just one of my thoughts had been a flash of lightning it could have reduced me to ashes. Poor mad soul!

[Les imbéciles! Eux, rire de moi! Eux si faibles, si communs, au cerveau si étroit; moi, dont l'esprit se noyait sur les limites de la création, qui étais perdu dans tous les mondes de la poésie, qui me sentais plus grand qu'eux tous, qui recevais des jouissances infinies et qui avais des extases célestes devant toutes les révélations intimes de mon âme! Moi qui me sentais grand comme le monde et qu'une seule de mes pensées, si elle eût été de feu comme la foudre, eût pu réduire en poussière; pauvre fou!][54]

The masochistic side of Gustave's character, too, had a corresponding sadistic side. Although his mother had always refused to meet Louise Colet, as Thibaudet recalls,[55] she was indignant about the brutal way in which he abandoned her. Gustave himself told the Goncourts that she never forgave her son's callousness toward his lover, the memory of which remained like a wound inflicted on her sex.

It has already been suggested that the teachers and schoolmates of Gustave might also be those of Charles. Consequently, either it must be assumed that that particular class was in the habit of teasing pupils—in which case it is hard to understand why the teacher made Charles write out *"ridiculus sum"*—or we must conclude that in portraying Charles, Gustave was portraying himself.

Gustave's father is known to have had no time for literature: indeed, when his son once read one of his works to him, he actually fell asleep. And yet Flaubert describes him as being a *very sensitive* man. Could it be that Gustave actually chose the wrong moment to read to him? Perhaps his father was just tired, or perhaps the tone of his son's voice lulled him to sleep. This hypothesis should not cause any surprise, for the experienced masochist (and a reading of "La Personnalisation" in Sartre's *L'Idiot de la famille* shows that this is precisely what Flaubert was) has at his disposal a vast range of expedients, as refined as they are *innocent,* to ensure that he will be rejected.

Neither Charles nor Gustave was jealous by nature. Flaubert was far from perturbed by the insistence of his lovers' various admirers. In a letter to Louise Colet, written in the late summer of 1846, he asks her about Victor Cousin: "Why do you so coldly reject that nice Philosopher, who is well aware of this and reproaches you for it? Do not neglect your friends; treat them as you always used to [Pourquoi repousses-tu si durement ce bon Philosophe qu'il s'en aperçoit et t'en fait des reproches? Ne néglige pas tes amis; sois avec eux comme tu étais auparavant]."[56]

Seven years later, when talking about Louis Bouilhet, his attitude has not changed: "Oh, you should love poor Bouilhet, for his love for you is touching—it has touched and saddened me [Ah, aime-le, ce pauvre Bouilhet, car il t'aime d'une façon touchante et qui m'a touché, navré]."[57] Is this evidence that the writer and Charles Bovary shared the same tastes? Flaubert seems to have outdone even Emma's husband.

A letter to Louis Bouilhet leaves us with little doubt on the subject. It was discovered at Chantilly in the Spehlberch de Lovenjoul collection, and published in its entirety only in the Pléiade edition of the *Correspondance*. On 15 January 1850 Gustave was in Cairo, where he had just celebrated his twenty-eighth birthday and returned from a visit to the pyramids with Maxime du Camp. He was both fascinated and perturbed by Egypt. In his notebooks, *Voyage en Orient*,[58] devoted to this part of his travels, the word "mélancholie" often appears as a counterpoint to the numerous descriptions of encounters, both heterosexual and homosexual. Scenes of violence and cruelty abound. His friend Bouilhet is given a much more explicit account of the events remarked upon in Gustave's diaries.

TO LOUIS BOUILHET

Cairo, 15 January 1850

My dear old friend, I received your long-awaited letter at midday today. I was moved to my very entrails. *It made me wet.* Ah, how I think of you, dear fellow. How often I think of you every day and how much I miss you! You may well be missing me, but I'm missing you, too. As I walk along the streets, nose in the air, looking up at the blue sky and at the *moucharabis*[59] of the houses and the minarets covered with birds, I dream of you. . . .

By the time we see each other again, so many days will have gone by, so many things will have happened. Will we still be the same? Will nothing have changed in the communion of our souls? . . .

I often go to the Turkish baths. . . . We haven't seen any dancing girls yet. They are all in exile in Upper Egypt. The beautiful brothels of Cairo have also disappeared. But we have had dancing men. Oh! Oh! Oh! . . .

As dancers, imagine two scoundrels, quite ugly but charming in their corruption, in the intentional degradation of their glances and the femininity of their movements, their eyes painted with antimony and wearing women's clothes. . . .

By that, I mean that they never smile. The effect is produced by the gravity of the head in contrast to the lascivious movements of the body. Sometimes they lie flat on their backs, like a woman lying down ready to be fucked. . . .

All this is fairly well accepted here. One admits one's sodomy openly and talks about it at table. Sometimes, someone tries to deny it, but then everybody begins shouting at him and he ends up confessing it. Since we are traveling for the sake of our education and are on a government mission, we thought it our duty to abandon ourselves to this style of ejaculation. . . .

It is practiced in the public baths. You book a bath (5 francs, which includes the masseurs, a pipe, coffee, and towels) and then stuff the boy in one of the rooms. The bath boys, by the way, are all *bardaches*.[60] The last masseurs, those who come to rub you down when it's all over, are usually rather nice young men. We saw one in a place quite near our hotel. I booked the bath *just for myself* and went there. The scoundrel wasn't there that day. . . .

It's all so voluptuous and full of sweet melancholy. . . .

Max[ime] got himself polluted the other day in one of the deserted quarters beneath the ruins, and he really enjoyed it. But enough of this lubricity.

My dear boy, I really long to embrace you. How pleased I shall be to see your face again. . . .

Go to see my mother often; keep up her morale; write to her when she is away from home; the poor woman needs it. That would be an act of great charity and it will allow you to discover in her the chaste expansion of a kindly, upright nature. Ah, dear fellow, if it weren't for her and you, I should hardly think about my country, my home. . . .

In the evening, when you are at home and the verses won't come and you think of me, when you are bored and resting your elbow on the table, take a sheet of paper and write down everything, everything that comes into your head. I devoured your letter when it came and have read it several times. Right now, I imagine you in your nightshirt sitting by the fire. You are too hot and are looking down at your pri . . . By the way, remember to write "cul" with an "l" and not "cu." The mistake shocked me.[61]

Over to you, my sturdy fellow.

Your old friend.

Caire, 15 janvier 1850

Ce matin à midi, cher et pauvre vieux, j'ai reçu ta bonne et longue lettre, tant désirée. Elle m'a remué jusqu'aux entrailles. *J'ai mouillé.* Comme je pense à toi, va! inestimable bougre! combien de fois par jour je t'évoque et que je te regrette! Si tu trouves que je te manque, tu me manques aussi. Et marchant le nez en l'air dans les rues, en regardant le ciel bleu, les moucharabis des maisons et les minarets couverts d'oiseaux, je rêve à ta personne . . .

Quand nous nous reverrons, il aura passé beaucoup de jours, je veux dire beaucoup de choses. Serons-nous toujours les mêmes, n'y aura-t-il rien de changé dans la communion de nos êtres . . . ? Je fréquente fort les bains turcs . . . Nous n'avons pas encore vu de danseuses. Elles sont toutes en Haute-Egypte, exilées. Les beaux bordels n'existent plus non plus au Caire . . . Mais nous avons eu les danseurs. Oh! Oh! Oh! . . .

Comme danseurs, figure-toi deux drôles passablement laids, mais charmant de corruption, de dégradation intentionnelle dans le regard et de féminité dans les mouvements, ayant les yeux peints avec de l'antimoine, et habillés en femmes . . .

J'entends par là qu'ils ne sourient point. L'effet résulte de la gravité de la tête en opposition avec les mouvements lascifs du corps. Quelquefois ils se reversent tout à fait sur le dos par terre, comme une femme qui se couche pour se faire baiser . . .

Ici c'est très bien porté. On avoue sa sodomie et on en parle à table d'hôte. Quelquefois on nie un petit peu, tout le monde alors vous engueule et ça finit par s'avouer. Voyageant pour notre instruction et chargés d'une mission par le gouvernement nous avons regardé comme de notre devoir de nous livrer à ce mode d'éjaculation . . .

C'est aux bains que cela se pratique. On retient le bain pour soi (5/Fr.., y compris les masseurs, la pipe, le café, le linge) et on enfile son gamin dans une des salles. Tu sauras du reste que tous les garçons de bains sont bardaches. Les derniers masseurs, ceux qui viennent vous frotter quand tout est fini, sont ordinairement de jeunes garçons assez gentils. Nous en avisâmes un dans un établissement tout proche de chez nous. Je fis retenir le bain *pour moi seul*. J'y allai. Le drôle était absent ce jour-là! . . . C'est très voluptueux et d'une mélancholie douce . . .

Max[ime] s'est fait polluer l'autre jour dans des quartiers déserts sous des décombres et a beaucoup joui. Assez de lubricités.

Pauvre cher bougre, j'ai bien envie de t'embrasser. Je serai content quand je reverrai ta figure . . .

Va voir ma mère souvent, soutiens-la, écris-lui quand elle sera absente, la pauvre femme en a besoin. Tu feras là un acte de haut évangélisme et comme étude, tu y verras l'expansion pudique d'une bonne et droite nature. Ah, vieux bardache, sans elle et toi je ne penserais guère a ma patrie, je veux dire à ma maison . . .

Le soir, quand tu es rentré, que les strophes ne vont pas, que tu penses à moi, et que tu t'ennuies, appuyé du bout du coude sur la table, prends un morceau de papier et envoie-moi tout, tout. J'ai mangé ta lettre et l'ai relue plus d'une fois. En ce moment, j'ai l'aperception de toi en chemise auprès de ton feu, ayant trop chaud et contemplant ton vi. A propos, écris donc cul avec un *l* et non *cu*. Ça m'a choqué . . .

A toi, mon solide

Ton vieux

Pederasty, sexual ambiguity, "corruption . . . degradation . . . sweet melancholy": the expression "Max s'est fait polluer" is an allusion not only to ejaculation but also to contamination, pollution. Then, at the end, Gustave mentions his friend—the "vieux bardache"—and his own mother in the same breath, and almost compares him with her. Flaubert wrote to Chantepie: "I often felt madness coming on [J'ai souvent senti la folie me venir]."[62]

Insatiability

"A lot of eating is done in Flaubert's novels [On mange beaucoup dans les romans de Flaubert]," remarked Jean-Pierre Richard, who was overwhelmed by so much orality.[63] From what has already been seen of the capacious Norman stomachs in *Madame Bovary*, he was not at all wrong. *Salammbô* and *Hérodias* also abound with Carthaginian and Judaean banquets, not to mention the absurd meals in *Bouvard et Pécuchet* and the *diners mondains* in *L'Education sentimentale:* "The table always appears as a meeting place, almost a place of communion among people. . . . Like another Moloch, Flaubert pounces greedily upon all sorts of nourishment, material and spiritual, so as to devour it alive."[64] "There is something so raw about it that it gives the spirit cannibal appetites. He falls upon it to devour and assimilate it [Elles ont quelque chose de si cru que cela donne à l'esprit des appetits de cannibale. Il se précipite dessus pour les dévorer, les assimiler]."[65] The eschatological insatiability of *Bouvard et Pécuchet* has a precedent in the appetites of Saint Anthony's pig:

I shall run, gallop, and swallow sleeping grass snakes as I pass by, devour fledglings that have fallen from their nests, and crouching hares; I shall frighten whole cities and devour the children at the gates. . . . I shall rummage in graves and eat monarchs rotting in their coffins, and their liquefied flesh will drip from my jaws.

[Je courrai, je galoperai, j'avalerai en passant les couleuvres qui dorment, les petits oiseaux tombés de leur nid, les lièvres tapis; j'épouvanterai les villes, sur les portes je dévorerai les enfants . . . Je fouillerai les tombeaux pour manger dans leur cercueils les monarques en pourriture et leur chair liquifiée s'écoulera de ma bouche.][66]

Is the first ideal hunger an attempt to bridle the frenzy of the second one? Reading, knowing, perceiving, and understanding are basically ways of eating with one's eyes, mashing, chewing, digesting, transforming: "Let us absorb the objective so that it may flow inside us [Absorbons l'objectif, et qu'il circule en nous]." Greed and its disturbing effects seem to be a major preoccupation in Gustave's life: "Isn't life just continuous indigestion? [La vie n'est-elle pas une indigestion continuelle?]."[67]

The mark of oral tragedy is impressed on all of his manifestations of love and passion. Flaubert's characters know only a selfish form of love: they are deaf to the other person's needs and suffer from a ravenous hunger that consumes.[68]

Flaubert's illness was once thought to be epilepsy, although Dr. René Dumesnil was inclined toward another hypothesis.[69] It was later diagnosed as hysterical epilepsy or, as Sartre called it, hysteria *tout court*. Like Dostoyevsky?[70]

W. Ronald D. Fairbairn had an important insight: while the sexuality of the hysteric is essentially extremely oral, his fundamental orality is, so to speak, extremely genital.[71] Gustave always felt an urgent need for a generous breast that would restore his faith in life, and his search never ceased: "I went for a swim in the Red Sea. It was one of the most voluptuous pleasures I have ever experienced; I splashed around in waves that felt like a thousand liquid bosoms passing over my entire body [J'ai pris un bain de mer dans la Mer Rouge. Ça a été un des plaisirs les plus voluptueux de ma vie; je me suis roulé dans les flots comme sur mille tétons liquides qui m'auraient parcouru tout le corps]." It was a need for fusion, for paradisiacal, primitive satiety: "I have never loved you so much, oceans of cream flooded my soul [Je ne t'ai jamais tant aimée, des océans de crème inondaient mon âme]," he wrote to Louise Colet.[72]

Yet this feeling of fullness was not stable: "It is strange to think that I was born with so little faith in happiness [C'est étrange de penser que je suis né avec si peu de foi dans le bonheur]." The invidious poison, when uncontrolled (and undoubtedly sanctioned by the literary fashions of the time), rises up from the roots of anger to putrefy. Referring to one of his characters, Flaubert wonders, "Had he never rested his head on the breast of a daughter of Eve? Had he never felt himself slowly dissolving in her love, like a tender plant rotting in the warm rain of a storm? [Celui-là n'avait donc jamais posé sa tête sur le sein d'une fille d'Eve? Ne s'était-il pas senti dissoudre avec lenteur dans son amour pour elle, comme une petite plante qui se pourrit sous la pluie chaude de l'orage?]."[73]

If the source of life is steeped in mortal hatred, all that is left is despair: "When I was still very young, I had a total premonition of what my life would be like. It was as if the nauseous smell of something cooking was coming in through an air vent. You don't need to taste the food to know that it will make you vomit [J'ai eu tout jeune le pressentiment de ce que serait toute ma vie. C'était comme une odeur de cuisine nauséabonde qui s'échappe par un soupirail. On n'a pas besoin d'en avoir mangé pour savoir qu'elle est à faire vomir]."[74]

It was always this nausea that carried Flaubert to new lands. In his correspondence and travel diaries, Gustave shows that he was never able to enjoy the present—satisfaction always lay in the future, in things yet unattained. Maupassant said that Flaubert was able to judge only from a distance; Richard added that he was affected by a contagious disease. His illness was bulimia: "What I need is digestion and appetite together, for I am distressed when I am replete and yet constantly devoured by the need to gorge myself. Here I am, full to the brim, my stomach stretched to the bursting point, and yet I am hungry [Il me faudrait ensemble la digestion et l'appetit, car je me désole d'être repu, et je suis continuellement dévoré par le besoin de me repaître. Me voilà gorgé jusqu'au larynx, la peau de mon ventre est tendu, et pourtant j'ai faim]."[75] *Bouvard et Pécuchet* also represents his sublimated, obstinate desire to establish a relationship with mother earth, which seduces but then betrays and rejects on contact.

Justin and Justine

Flaubert was not quite seventeen when he wrote *Mémoires d'un fou*. It is here that he describes his first meeting with Elise Schlésinger, who was to be the model for Madame Arnoux in *L'Education sentimentale*—the revered but unreachable woman par excellence. Gustave writes of his perturbation on seeing her while she was breast-feeding: "Oh! What a singular ecstasy overcame me at the sight of that breast; how I devoured it with my eyes, how I longed just to touch that bosom! It seemed to me that if I had brushed it with my lips, my teeth would have sunk into it with anger. My heart melted with delight at the thought of the voluptuous pleasures which that kiss would bring [Oh, la singulière extase où me plongeait la vue de ce sein; comme je le dévorais des yeux, comme j'aurais voulu seulement toucher cette poitrine! Il me semblait que si j'eusse posé mes lévres, mes dents l'auraient mordue de rage; et mon coeur se fondait en délices en pensant aux voluptés que donnerait ce baiser]."[76]

Without any apparent logic, Flaubert had earlier described two dreams (frightful visions, as he called them), which may be seen to represent some of these anxieties. The first dream is full of strange figures of various sizes: they all have bristly black beards and carry steel blades between their teeth. These ogrelike creatures surround his cradle, gnash their teeth horribly, and stare at him "out of wide lidless eyes [avec des grands yeux fixes et sans paupières]." They also leave bloodstains on everything they touch: "It felt as if the house was coming away from its foundations, as if it were being levered up [Il me sembla alors que la maison se levait de ses fondements, comme si un levier l'eût soulevée]." They stare at him for a long time and then move away; he then notices that they all have bleeding sores on one side of their face. They start eating bread, which exudes drops of blood as they break it: "And then they all let out a laugh that sounded like a death rattle [Et ils se mirent à rire comme le râle d'un mourant]." When these creatures have disappeared, the child feels as if he "has been eating flesh [d'avoir mangé de la chair]." He then hears a long, drawn-out wail, "like a weird song that hissed as it tore open my breast with a dagger [comme une bizarre chanson dont chaque sifflement me déchirait la poitrine avec un stylet]."[77] The lidless eyes, the shrill cry, the weird, deathly song—all of these images were to be reincarnated in that part of Charles which is symbolized by the blind beggar of the coaches. Recurring nightmares point to a particularly vigorous unresolved conflict.

The sequel to this dream is no less terrifying. This time the child is older and is walking with his mother along the river when he suddenly notices that she has fallen in and mysteriously disappeared below the surface: "I saw the water bubbling; the circles widened out and disappeared, . . . and then all I could hear was the sound of the water as it passed through the rushes and bent the reeds [Je vis l'eau écumer, des cercles s'agrandir et disparaître . . . et puis je n'entendis plus que le bruit de l'eau qui passait entre les joncs et faisait ployer les roseaux]."[78] He hears his mother crying for help but does not move, for he senses that some irresistible force keeps him anchored to the spot. "The clear water flowed, and the voice that I could hear coming from the bottom of the river overwhelmed me with despair and anger [L'eau coulait, coulait limpide, et cette voix que j'entendais du fond du fleuve m'abîmait de désespoir et de rage]."[79] Here, too, his love and the desire to save and repair seem to be overcome by destructive fury, the force of the water as it bends the reeds. This dream has the same unconscious meaning as the nightmare that haunts Charles after Emma's death.

Gustave's anxious orality is evident in both nightmares: the blade of steel that the creatures hold between their teeth evokes the grip produced by the act of biting (one might tentatively suggest that before teething the inside of the child's mouth felt as though it were composed of two blades). Such cannibalistic anger (the sensation of having eaten flesh) is also present in the whirlpool of the later dream. The ripples beneath which the woman vanishes and the circles that widen out and disappear are signs of a tragic swallowing. Flaubert's tremendous capability for enthusiasm, his grandiose visions and epic gestures, what has been called his taste for the exorbitant, conceal his terrible passivity, his greedy desire for milk, attention, and love, as well as the exclusive nature of his relationships with friends. When Alfred Le Poittevin married, Flaubert remarked: "That's another one I've lost [En voilà encore un perdu pour moi]."[80] All such characteristics underlay his fever for travel, the tormented way in which he attempted to enjoy life, success, and women—whether prostitutes or oriental princesses. Brombert summed him up as follows: "He prefers everything that is excessive."[81] His insatiability is morbid because it is accompanied by a sense of death. *Mémoires d'un fou,* like much of his work, is soaked with the blood that Gustave shed in his role as Avenging Angel.

What tempers his destructiveness is his great creative ambition as well as the benevolent presence of Madonna figures such as Elise Schlésinger. When Emma has consummated her adulterous affair with Rodolphe, she also feels the need for protective, understanding Madonna figures: "She spoke of her own mother and of his, . . . 'I am sure that up there, together, they approve of our love' [Elle l'entretenait de sa mère, à elle, et de sa mère, à lui, . . . 'Je suis sûre que là-haut, ensemble, elles approuvent notre amour']" (182/204).

On the one hand, Flaubert's obsessive idea of living like a hermit represents an escape from the concrete possibilities of his longings, of his desire for self-annihilation in the object; on the other hand, it is a refuge where he can give free rein to all his fantasies: "you deny yourself meat, wine, steam baths, slaves, and honors; but how you let your imagination offer you banquets, perfumes, naked women, and applauding crowds! Your chastity is nothing but a subtler form of corruption [Tu te prives de viandes, de vin, d'étuves, d'esclaves et d'honneurs; mais comme tu laisses ton imagination t'offrir des banquets, des parfums, des femmes nues et des foules applaudissantes! Ta chasteté n'est qu'une corruption plus subtile]."[82]

The intense need for mystical union that he expresses in the project for a work called *La Spirale,* "a metaphysical novel with apparitions [un roman métaphysique et à apparitions], can also be traced in his personal crises and in those of his characters (including Emma). It is a leitmotif in his *Correspondance,* too— one that in 1875 would lead him to conclude his *Tentation de Saint Antoine* with the cry "to be matter! [être la matière!]."[83]

However, the law of retaliation requires that the fantasies of devouring find their contrast in corresponding fantasies of being devoured, the terrible threat of a primitive mother who denies herself but is demanding: "the past devours me [le passé me devore]."[84] Besides, doesn't Justin, who provides Emma with poison, bear the same name as Flaubert's mother, Anne-Justine-Caroline Fleuriot? "Justin" and "Justine" were names that had been handed down from generation to generation in Gustave's family: his maternal great-grandfather, a lawyer in Pont l'Evêque, was called Nicolas-Guillaume-Justin, while Gustave's maternal grandmother's name was Charlotte-Justine-Camille.

Gustave would have to face the Oedipal triangle with the burden of this conflict on his shoulders, with the unconscious conviction of a paradise both lost and destroyed, though uncertain whether this was through his own greed or his mother's voracious aridity. The conflict with his father and the grim atmosphere of the corpse-filled Hôpital Majeur de Rouen could only increase his anxiety, horror, and disgust.

According to Freud, the moral masochist's fantasies hide an underlying desire to have passive feminine sexual relations.[85] Flaubert's works frequently contain images in which masochistic tactics and perverse desires are fused—to be seen, for example, not only in the servile role of many of his female characters but in the characters of his young men in love. *The Servant,* the most "Hegelian" of Joseph Losey's films, provides one of the finest illustrations of this technique: the servant insinuates himself into his master's house and uses his passive dependence to corrupt him, reverse the terms of the relationship and take control of the situation. This is the same behavior as that of Ernest, as described by the fifteen-year-old Gustave in *Passion et vertu;* while a similar stratagem appears in *Novembre* and in *L'Education sentimentale*: to desire a married woman, and to this end make friends with her husband, shake him warmly by the hand, laugh at his puns, sympathize when business is bad and run errands for him.[86] In *L'Education sentimentale,* the same expedient is used by Frédéric Moreau with Arnoux, in other words by Gustave with Monsieur Schlésinger, "my venerable Père Maurice [mon vénérable père Maurice]."[87] In *Madame Bovary* Léon offers to run errands for Charles and for his birthday buys him a fine, turquoise-colored phrenological model of a head.

Yet challenges are repaid with insecurity: Flaubert's pathological idiosyncrasy for *la bêtise humaine* (which he also recognized as being his own *bêtise*) and his excessive preoccupation with style, which stupefied the Goncourts and left Turgenev wide-eyed with astonishment, are but a measure of his fragility—the obsessive result of his anxieties.[88]

It was these anxieties, which he was quite unable to limit, that kept him wavering between living a life of pleasure and ascetic withdrawal: "I love debauchery and live like a monk [la débauche me plaît et je vis comme un moine]."[89] Again it was these anxieties which caused him to keep due distance from women, even though he showed himself able to love some with rapture and sensuality and others with tenacity and devotion. Even his relationship with Louise Colet was a basically epistolary passion kept alight by the very distance that lay between them. His anxieties did, indeed, eventually prevail, and he ended his life in solitude.

Although it caused him suffering, renunciation seems also to have appeased him: when living in Croisset, with his writing, his books, and his pipes, Gustave no longer suffered the lack of a mother figure and was to realize his childhood dream of having a family—composed of himself, his mother, and his young niece, Caroline.

Oedipus and Orestes

Flaubert was a fascinated reader of Sade, and fetishist tendencies have often been observed in him. He was morbidly attracted by a pair of red satin shoes in a shop window and by Louise Colet's slippers. A similar tendency can be glimpsed in the character of Justin, Emma Bovary's little slave. Charles himself collects locks of Emma's hair, as was doubtless the custom of the time, but he also keeps Emma's clothes and shuts himself away in his dressing room to look at them.

These are facets of Flaubert's complex personality that might be of no more interest than others—his blatant onanism, for example—if it were not for their repercussions: "In the end, driven by some mystical impulse, the hero wants to castrate himself. At the age of nineteen, when I was living in Paris and in the thick of all my troubles, I felt the same urge (I'll show you the little shop in rue Vivienne where I stopped one evening and was intensely overcome by this dominant idea) at a time when I didn't see a woman for two whole years [A la fin, le héros veut se châtrer, par une espèce de manie mystique. J'ai eu, au milieu de mes ennuis de Paris, à dix-neuf ans, cette envie (je te montrerai dans la rue Vivienne une boutique devant laquelle je me suis arrêté un soir, pris par cette idée avec une intensité impérieuse), alors que je suis resté deux ans entiers sans voir de femme]."[90]

According to Freud, fetishism is a way of dealing with the inability to consciously accept the idea that some human beings lack a penis and, following a typically infantile form of reasoning, must therefore be thought of as if they had been castrated. The implicit threat is obvious: if women have been castrated, then the same can happen to anybody. In fetishism there is a displacement of erotic feelings away from the genitals of the loved one onto some other part of the body or an object belonging to her (in Justin's case, for instance, Emma's shoes) in a symbolic attempt to restore the missing phallus. So much for the formula of early psychoanalysis.

These tendencies have subsequently come to be seen as the negative side of other formations based upon anxieties of an almost psychotic nature, such as those mentioned by Gustave. It may be said that through perversion Flaubert was attempting an authentic, spontaneous therapy against the kind of anxiety that would otherwise lead him to madness.[91]

Sartre and Marthe Robert emphasized Gustave's Oedipal problems,[92] yet the matricidal obsession (which also generated *Madame Bovary*) cannot be explained entirely with reference to the Oedipus complex. In an early essay, Ernest Jones accepted the theory that the story of Orestes is in reality only that of Oedipus under a different name, but the theory was destined to be short-lived.[93]

Before going any further, it is worth telling those few readers who tend to misunderstand such observations that I personally do not find it proper to consider Flaubert exclusively in relation to his pathology: a genius cannot be portrayed as the sum of his childhood conflicts (nor should I wish to be accused of so crude a simplification). Moreover, I do not think we should allow ourselves to give in to the temptation to see Flaubert as a frightened *bourgeois révolté* who took refuge in art, as Maurice Nadeau seems to fear.[94] On the other hand, it would not be wise to ignore these very serious conflicts in real terms, if only because of the light they throw on the later Flaubert, the author of *Bouvard et Pécuchet*. It seems useless to deny that this literary turning point, which would not only father Joyce and the modern novel but also provide one of the crucial keys to our society, is related to tensions that lead other people to madness.

Behind Gustave's great admiration for his father—or, rather, existing alongside it—lay a strong sense of hostility. The episode in which Bovary tries to straighten Hippolyte's crippled leg echoes Flaubert's father's attempt to cure the deformed foot of a little girl, who lay in a coma for several months with her foot in an iron harness.

Flaubert's rancour, however, was due not only to the Oedipal contrast (in the sense that became popular with the growth of psychoanalysis) but also to the fact that Achille-Cléophas had not succeeded in becoming a valid model for his son—he had not represented a pole of attraction to counteract Gustave's urgent need for the maternal care of which he had been deprived.

Sartre describes Flaubert's father as a "présence écrasante,"[95] the "terrible docteur" who burdened his wife with the guilt of being the mother of *morituri*—a paternal influence to which Flaubert's passivity, femininity, and vocation as hermit-novelist have been attributed (although Victor Brombert wonders whether this influence was really so pernicious). According to this theory, the materialistic father is supposed to have hampered his son's idealistic aspirations. And yet behind all such images lies another, quite different one—that of a man of great sensitivity, intelligence, and subtlety, whose relationship with his children was manipulated by his wife.[96]

With surprising ingenuousness, Sartre states the very opposite: "She loved him too loyally to attempt to maneuver him," but then he goes on to reconstruct a life of Caroline Fleuriot that contradicts this interpretation. Madame Flaubert does not once take her children's side against her husband or use her tenderness to mitigate the authority of the paterfamilias. She is a wife more than a mother, accepting her children as a gift of God for love of her husband and out of duty, and when God takes them away from her she sheds no tears. Sartre then hastens to produce some sociological information: "Since at the beginning of the last century children dropped dead like flies, parents were advised not to love them too much."[97]

This unconditional surrender to her husband (Caroline had already decided before marrying that she would comply with all his wishes) should make us pause for thought, for it is impressively similar to Charles's essential attitude toward Emma. This sort of behavior tends to manifest a hidden desire to exercise omnipotent control over the relationship. Lacking the strength to act maturely and on an equal footing, the subject tends to compensate unconsciously. Sartre-as-diagnostician does not suspect Caroline of using her docility to manipulate the relationship between her husband and her children—yet the idea is by no means unfounded, which Sartre-as-writer seems to have sensed as far back as when he wrote *L'Etre et le néant*.[98] By apparently annihilating her own personality in that of her husband, by apparently canceling out her presence between him and the children, she succeeds in estranging them from him, thereby creating a terrible ogre who was to be feared rather than loved. Her docility was a means of arbitrating the situation.

The situation can be better clarified by further reference to information contained in *L'Idiot de la famille*. Caroline the mother-sister who was not responsible in the presence of her husband hides the permanently depressed, possessive hypochondriac: "For eight months she had been certain that she was suffering from breast cancer! [Depuis huit mois, elle croyait avoir un cancer au sein!]."[99] When her husband died, she almost broke off relations with her son Achille.

Sartre describes her as a woman who (again like Charles Bovary) never allows herself to show either anger or jealousy, not even when her husband leaves her standing on the street with her children while he stops to pay his respects to a former mistress. "Caroline's personality was such that she was untouched by joy or sorrow unless they came directly from Achille-Cléophas."[100]

The fact that some children become blind, that they repress what they see or feel (with the help of idealization), might find confirmation in the case of Sartre's mother, whom Sartre himself describes as a compliant mother-sister, while her "daughter-in-law," Simone de Beauvoir, describes her as having a strong, manipulative personality.

"Caroline lived *in her love*, which was her constant strength, her fixed point and her nourishment." The reward for such devotion soon follows: "in the rigorous life of a head physician, love certainly occupied second place."[101] Thus, the picture of Caroline is that of an immature woman in need of affection who, first from her father and later from her husband, demanded, as she would from a mother, a primitive and total protection that might satisfy a need that had not only remained unfulfilled but was also probably laden with guilt. She must certainly have added to her own self-reproach the reproach of her father, who seems never to have forgiven her for having caused her mother's death during childbirth.

The tragedy in the life of this woman would seem to have been the loss of her mother at birth, which must have led her to feel unconsciously rejected and to assume that she therefore had only duties, without suspecting that she also had rights. In such cases, the process of mourning can be extremely dramatic and lead to serious psychic disorders. How could she express her anger toward her husband for having neglected her and gone to talk to his former mistress if she felt that she was nothing more than an appendage? Sartre says that she could have died of jealousy a thousand times without any of her children noticing it. Perhaps he is guilty of naïveté once more. Is it really likely that anything could have been hidden from the sensitivity of a child like Gustave? One instantly recalls the words written several decades later to describe Charles Bovary's mother: "She had suffered so much, without complaint, at first, when she saw him chasing after every slut in the village [Elle avait tant souffert, sans se plaindre, d'abord, quand elle le voyait courir après toutes les gotons du village]" (4/38). The repressed rage that smoldered behind the mother's pitiful and indifferent mask quite probably fueled her son's nightmares as well as providing the element he transfused into his sadistic queens and the greedy, castrating women of his novels.

Gustave Flaubert, then, had ambiguous images of the parents whom he should try to resemble and he identified badly with both of them (after all, he imagined Louise Colet as a "sublime hermaphrodite" and Montaigne as his "father-nurse").[102] The example of a conjugal relationship that he had before him may have conformed to certain contemporary bourgeois patterns, but it also had a singular sadomasochistic structure.

In his search for love, Gustave always had to reckon with his pathologist father, who dissected corpses at the Hospice d'Humanité, who threatened him, who did not understand him—"he understood nothing of my idiom [il n'entendait rien à mon idiome]"[103]—and did not give him support, and with his mother, whose appearance of submissiveness to the point of masochism masked a cold and avid nature. In the midst of these contrasting feelings, he was never really able to know himself: in his final isolation at Croisset he was left with nothing but his struggle with the artifices of style, which borders on the psychotic in

Bouvard et Pécuchet,[104] and the fight against the threat posed by the hated *bêtise* concealed in his own language: "their stupidity is my own; it is killing me [leur bêtise c'est la mienne, j'en crève]."[105] It was an obsession that would persecute him to the grave.

This perfectionism, which brought its incomparable results, was also the means by which Gustave used the alchemy of words in his attempt to circumscribe "the necropolis, a thousand inner ceremonies of mourning, . . . despair . . . nothingness . . . the tedium of existence [la nécropole . . . les mille funérailles intérieures . . . le désespoir . . . le néant . . . la lassitude de l'existence]." In 1875, Flaubert's love for his niece Caroline brought him to financial ruin. In an effort to save her husband from bankruptcy, he would eventually lose all of his property. This is yet another episode in common with the life of Charles Bovary: we should not exclude the possibility that Flaubert had unconsciously foreseen it.

For Derek Jacobi, Hamlet, and Claudius

The Barbarous Scythian

An Essay on *King Lear*

When it comes to poetry and art, things have a different complexion. . . . Philoctetes, Ajax, Heracles achieve tragedy in moments of madness; Lear and Ophelia are actually mad, while Hamlet feigns madness. Don Quixote is almost a typical schizophrenic. . . . In these areas the sufferer is often represented as both sufferer and symbol of a profound human mystery. —KARL JASPERS

Neither Letters nor Words

Gregory Kozintsev began taking notes on *King Lear* around 1941 on the occasion of his production of the play at the Gorki Theatre. He took them up again from 1968 to 1972, while he was preparing the film version starring Yuri Yarvet in the leading role. These notes then appeared periodically in the Russian cinema journal *Isskustvo Kino.* Although he had been fascinated by Peter Brook's production of the tragedy for the National Theatre when the British company had toured the Soviet Union, he was not actually able to discuss *Lear* with Brook until 1967. The English director had just completed his *Marat–Sade.* Kozintsev had come to London after a visit to Japan, which had left him haunted by the memory of Toshiro Mifune's eyes and of the Zen Garden of the fifteenth-century Ryonaji monastery: "neither letters nor words can capture the true essence of nature."[1]

Brook had just published *The Empty Space,*[2] and Kozintsev was to entitle his diary *The Space of Tragedy,* almost suggesting a link with the title of his friend's book.

Søren Kierkegaard began one of his books with the description of a tombstone he had seen somewhere in England, bearing the laconic inscription "the most unfortunate."[3] Kozintsev himself quotes Kierkegaard: "All that I see is empty, everything I live by is empty, everything in which I move is empty." The Russian director continues:

> Working on a Shakespearean tragedy reminds one of archeology; the search is always going deeper, beneath the limits of the top layers; the whole is usually reconstructed from fragments. But the strange thing is that the deeper you dig, the more contemporary everything that comes to the surface seems as it reveals its significance.
>
> The fragment relates to the past but it is as if the plate was broken today; it is possible that just such a plate will be broken tomorrow.
>
> One must show not some single unifying theme in the work (there isn't one), but the path of exploration into human nature and the process of history—man making history and history making man.[4]

Even if there is no ultimate interpretation of *King Lear,* the play probably does have a unifying theme—the empty space, the sweetest melancholy, the tragic space of the most unfortunate king.[5]

Commonplaces

It is time to return to the subject of stereotypes. More than most other Shakespearean plays, except perhaps *Othello, King Lear* has given rise to enduring commonplaces. *King Lear* is the tragedy of horrible "filial ingratitude," the king is a grandiose figure, and most of the characters are seen as being set in contrast with one another and placed on opposite sides of a well-defined divide. On one side stand the "good" and "loyal" characters who love and support the old king: first and foremost Cordelia, the "sweet and adamantine" daughter, who has been compared with Christ on more than one occasion.[6] "Noble" Kent and the Fool unfailingly figure among the good.

On the other side are the "evil" characters who bring the old king to ruin—the ungrateful daughters, Goneril and Regan, and, most contemptible of all, in Andrew C. Bradley's opinion, the steward, Oswald. In the parallel subplot involving the Earl of Gloucester, Edgar, the legitimate son, naturally belongs in the ranks of the good, while Edmund, the bastard, is placed in the ranks of the evil.[7] Lear (or Leir, as it is spelled in the versions predating Shakespeare's play) and Cordelia (Cordeilla) have over the years been set apart from the other characters and, owing to the popularity of Shakespeare's work, have gradually acquired the autonomy of archetypal figures—or, rather, of figures traditionally associated with certain fixed characteristics or deeds. In such a way, they were made ready to enter the realm of fable and "point a moral," as William Bedell Stanford would put it.[8]

However, it could be suggested to those who prefer blunt simplicity that Lear's ruin is hastened ("caused" would be excessive) by "sweet" Cordelia and "noble" Kent, while the Fool is the king's chief tormentor. Yet such a statement will be seen to be as moralistic as it is Manichean. What is true of Flaubert's characters is probably true of all the great figures in literature, above all Shakespeare's: no one is all demon or all saint.

One particular question will be recurrent in this essay: Is Lear rash and overbearing because of his age, or are these personality traits? If they are, did they originate in his infancy and gradually reinforce themselves with the passing of time? His older daughters discuss the point:

Regan   'Tis the infirmity of his age.
        Yet he hath ever but slenderly known himself.
Goneril The best and soundest of his time has been but rash.
        (1.1.292–95)[9]

Psychoanalytic experience suggests that an adult who behaves like a child is enacting a behavioral pattern that he has never overcome. This is more or less the conclusion that Goneril comes to.

Another fact that clinical experience suggests we should not forget is that Lear's spoiled and overbearing attitudes are related to a fragility deriving from serious conflicts and anxieties. Old age very probably aggravates and brings to the surface conflicts and behavioral patterns that have earlier been kept under control or altogether concealed, for "nothing will come of nothing." The idea I intend to develop is that the king feels a desperate need for gratitude and love on the part of his daughters but that he cannot acknowledge this need. To feel need is humiliating for a king, and he is "every inch a king," even when he ironizes upon his own misfortunes.

That *King Lear* also represents a conflict between generations and the crisis of the aristocracy, and Goethe's belief that "every old man is a King Lear,"[10] are largely acceptable assertions. However, they should not be allowed to limit the possibilities of demonstrating my hypothesis.

Cordelia the Favorite

. . . whom Nature is ashamed,
Almost t'acknowledge hers.

Cordelia is Lear's favorite daughter, so much so that the king expressly plans to spend the last years of his life with her (1.1.124–25). Her sisters are well aware of this, and so is France (1.1.214–17, 291). Her father intends to give her a "more opulent" part of his kingdom than the parts set aside for his other daughters.[11] Even his manner of asking them in turn to express their love for him shows discrimination. He addresses Goneril somewhat coldly, calling her simply "our eldest born" (1.1.54), without adding a single word of tenderness; he shows Regan a little more affection, using the superlative "our dearest" (1.1.68). But when it comes to Cordelia, he uses a very different expression: "our joy" (1.1.82).

We are not actually told why Cordelia is the favorite, although some kind of conclusion might perhaps be drawn from the few clues available (Cordelia speaks no more than a hundred lines in the whole play). However, closer attention will paid to Cordelia's later demonstration of affection toward her father once the substrata of her father's mind have been probed a little more deeply.

The very idea of staging a love contest should make us stop to think. Lear invites his three daughters to declare publicly and unreservedly (before his courtiers, *vil razza dannata,* and follow-ing a fanfare) feelings that mature, sensitive people usually prefer to express in private, probably through attitudes or gestures rather than words. As a rule, true love tends to be declared in whispers; if we find ourselves shouting it from the rooftops, we usually sense that something is basically wrong.[12] Indeed, if we are required to be ostentatious, we sense that force is being used. After all, Cordelia's great appeal over the centuries derives from her resistance to her father's request, which tends to compel our sympathy.

Lear shows himself to be unaware of these simple truths. By staging a public competition (prizes and all) between his daugh-ters, he gives the impression of being a person who has probably never experienced the delicacy of genuine feelings of love. And even if he has, he was unable to *recognize* it for what it was. Any-one who needs emphasis or "fulsome excess" reveals an inability to appreciate the fundamental value of spontaneous demonstra-tions of affection.

The type of insensitivity Lear displays is symptomatic of a lack of affection during his childhood. A profound lack. Anyone who does not exercise discretion when dealing with others has usually not experienced discretion. Moreover, being a monarch at a time when this meant wielding almost absolute power must have made no small contribution to reinforcing in Lear the idea that the use of coercion to obtain demonstrations of love was some-thing entirely normal.

Goneril is unaware of the extent of her father's pathology, but she is clearly able to see that he is infantile. Regan does not appear to have such a firm understanding, but she imitates her sister in pleasing him. Cordelia is different. Cordelia, the favor-ite, feels threatened by the situation Lear has contrived. Yet in the past she must have known how to humor Lear's unhealthy need for self-esteem in order to become the darling daughter of a father so fragile, so utterly incapable of tolerating even indirect criticism, let alone reproaches.

If this hypothesis is mistaken, we would have to imagine *two* Lears: one who is able to maintain a genuine relationship with

Cordelia and one who is blind to the most blatant flattery—a somewhat improbable scenario. It must, then, be wondered why Cordelia suddenly changes her attitude. The answer may be (not least because of her age) that she is simply not mature enough to sense and thus find some way of tolerating the madness underlying her father's insistence on a public exhibition. His need to stage his daughters' testimony of love for all to hear—"which of you shall we say doth love us most?" (1.1.52)—makes her feel offended rather than sad or worried.

But this is surely not the whole story. On closer examination, Cordelia also shows herself to be jealous (a fact that traditional commonplace interpretations have ignored). Indeed, the jealousy she feels toward her sisters has by now become nothing less than an *idée fixe*. Nor should the possibility be excluded that her feeling worthy and deserving of love depends on her being the favorite. The favorite child frequently has fantasies about being an only child. It has been suggested that her jealousy of her sisters is an *idée fixe* because throughout the tragedy Cordelia appears to show implacable rancor toward them, and fear, feelings that seem to have their origins in the distant past.

In the first scene, the excessive flattery of Goneril and Regan disgusts the audience (especially if the director overdoes it). Yet it does not disgust Lear, who is the victim of his own long-standing greed and thus unable to distinguish between authenticity and falseness. He is incapable of making subtle distinctions, just like someone who is dying of thirst, or a drug addict suffering withdrawal symptoms.

Cordelia, by contrast, feels not so much disgust as *danger* when she hears her sisters' exaggerated praise. She does not think: Poor father! What manner of falseness must he put up with this time! Instead, after Goneril's speech, she asks herself: "What shall Cordelia speak? Love, and be silent" (1.1.63). And after Regan has spoken:

> Then poor Cordelia—
> And yet not so; since I am sure my love's
> More ponderous than my tongue. (1.1.77–79)

If sufficient attention is paid to Cordelia's asides, the idea occurs that during the contest she may have felt ill at ease and outdone precisely by her sisters' lack of finesse.

At first she feels impoverished; only after she has collected her thoughts does she declare herself to be not at all *poor*, but richer. It is as if an inner dialogue were taking place: one voice expresses fear and insecurity, the other is the voice of self-esteem and dignity.

Nobody would want to devalue the importance of a Cordelia who, out of a just sense of pride, refuses to descend to the level on which Lear wishes to place his daughters' feelings. To give but one example, John Holloway is absolutely right in stating that what Cordelia wants is for Lear to do "what it is a father's duty to do: not what it is *her* duty to do in return."[13] Since this side of Cordelia's character has been emphasized to the exclusion of all others, I feel almost obliged to demonstrate that there exists *another* Cordelia.

It has been suggested that she is worried about herself rather than about her deceived father. Yet it is clear from the very first scene that the kingdom has already been divided up and that the "more opulent" part is to be hers. Since she states that her own love is more "ponderous" than that of her sisters, it seems reasonable to assume that, in her own way, she is a woman who weighs her thoughts and affections. Cordelia's frequent, spontaneous talk of weights and measures and her habit of weighing up affections are worth consideration. "I return those duties back as are right fit" (1.1.97), she tells her father, and a little earlier: "I love your majesty / According to my bond, no more nor less" (1.1.92–93). This kind of obsession might well reveal deep-seated traits that surface only when she is a prey to anxiety. And it has been seen that the love contest has made her anxious.

Perhaps her concern for appearances at times of great emotional involvement reflects these particular aspects of her personality. "Be better suited" (4.6.7), she advises Kent just after the final reunion, while she asks the doctor who has found and helped the old king: "Is he arrayed?" (4.6.18). For such aid she had promised, perhaps somewhat exaggeratedly: "He that helps him, take all my outward worth" (4.3.10).

Yet something even more relevant must be remarked: Cordelia's attention is centered on her sisters and *only secondarily* on her father, both in the opening scene and in many of her subsequent appearances. Even when she worries about her father, she sees him as a *victim* of her sisters—in the following passage, for example:

> O my dear father! Restoration hang
> Thy medicine on my lips, and let this kiss
> Repair those violent harms that my two sisters
> Have in thy reverence made! (4.6.23–26)

The few tender, heartfelt sentences spoken by her during the final meeting with Lear are all accompanied by expressions of blame for Goneril and Regan, who are always a threatening presence in her mind.

Cordelia does not "suffer because of her sweetness," as one used to read in the popular Bell school editions published in the First World War period.[14] Are there sufficient indications to allow a bolder hypothesis about the thoughts that lie simmering below the surface? When her sisters show that they are able to satisfy their father's primitive need for praise and Lear publicly announces that his kingdom is to be divided among his three daughters, Cordelia does something to maintain her privileged place in her father's heart: she transforms her favored status into negative supremacy. If she cannot have all of her father's love, she must have all of his hatred.

Lear himself indicates this abrupt passage from love to hatred when telling Burgundy that Cordelia is "new adopted to our hate" (1.1.202). He disowns her, and is then immediately forced to adopt her! Shakespeare uses extraordinarily subtle devices to stress how much Lear cares for his favorite daughter even at the peak of his anger and vexation. The king speaks the following words to France so that he, too, might reject Cordelia:

> For you great king,
> I would not from your love make such a stray
> To match you where I hate, therefore beseech you
> T'avert your liking a more worthier way

Than on a wretch whom nature is ashamed
Almost t'acknowledge hers. (1.1.207–12)

Almost! Lear is a manipulator. Not only does he constantly play his daughters off against one another, but whenever he quarrels with one of them he always leans on a daughter who is absent.[15] In order to be able to take part in the dispute caused by her father, Cordelia seems obliged to construct a heroic image of herself.

From a rhetorical point of view, Goneril gives the "perfect" answer in the love contest. In an effort to outdo her, Regan comes up with declarations that seem more suited to describe a mystical relationship with God. And in order to steal the show (after all, her sisters have impressed their father), Cordelia has no choice but to change her tune altogether.[16] She might almost be said to shift from C major to A minor.

As is often the case with the youngest child, it is quite possible that Cordelia not only had to find her own personal ways of winning her father's affection but also had to construct unconscious techniques and expedients to oppose her rivals verbally— rivals who were intrusive not least because they were older. It is also quite likely that Cordelia, Lear's "joy," had learned to communicate well with Lear in private though not in public. Her first remarks are, however, extremely effective:

Lear   Now, our joy,
        Although our last and least, to whose young love
        The vines of France and milk of Burgundy
        Strive to be interested: what can you say to draw
        A third more opulent than your sisters? Speak.
Cordelia Nothing, my lord
Lear   Nothing?
Cordelia Nothing.
Lear   Nothing will come of nothing. Speak again.
Cordelia Unhappy that I am, I cannot heave
        My heart into my mouth. I love your majesty
        According to my bond, no more nor less.
Lear   How, how, Cordelia! Mend your speech a little
        Lest you may mar your fortunes.

Cordelia   Good my lord,
            You have begot me, bred me, loved me.
            I return those duties back as are right fit-
            Obey you, love you, and most honour you. (1.1.82–98)

Cordelia was born to a capricious, tyrannical father, to whom she
must have become attached as if to a mother. Throughout the
entire tragedy there is only one brief reference to the queen, in
one of Lear's imprecations; the three sisters are presented as
never having had a mother. Cordelia is intelligent and it is not
difficult for her to find extremely effective words. She devises a
very subtle comparison, for example, when it comes to demolish-
ing the rivals who have just proclaimed their total devotion to
their father:

    Sure I shall never marry like my sisters,
    To love my father all. (Q1.95–96)[17]

But this is not the truth. She is in fact a mere child and far from
being as her words depict her. Indeed, after her reconciliation
with Lear, she tells him that as soon as she was alone with her
husband she found herself longing for her father:

            O dear father,
        It is thy business that I go about;
        Therefore great France
        My mourning and importuned tears hath pitied. (4.3.23–26)

Paradoxically, Goneril and Regan had come closer to telling the
truth in their grandiloquent speeches. As the play develops, they
also show the prime importance of their attachment to Lear both
by continually leaving their husbands in the background and later
by sharing a lover.

Essentially, Cordelia appears to have feelings only for her family and regards everybody else with indifference.[18] Although
France and Burgundy have been at Lear's court for some time,
she is not interested in either of them. Burgundy turns out to be a
small-minded suitor with his sights set on her dowry, whereas
France is truly fascinated by Cordelia's personality and by her

reply to her father. It is consequently surprising that she should have kept them both waiting, on equal terms, for an answer. This appears to indicate that she did not care for either one or the other. She waits to be chosen. Perhaps she is only thinking of the fact that her father wants to end his days with her and thus satisfy what Freud would call her "Oedipal" demands (1.1.123–24).

Perhaps one should attempt to explain Cordelia's "heroic" behavior more fully. Lear has quite probably always made comparisons between one daughter and another (a pathology like his tends to be repetitive); Cordelia's feeling that she was the favorite might have enabled her either to deny or at least minimize these comparisons.[19] Everything in the love contest (so laden, above all, with material consequences) seems to suggest that this is the first public comparison that Lear has arranged. It may be this very fact that obliges Cordelia to put a brutal end to all illusions. Her worried reactions suggest that the contest has had the effect of a violent laceration, a sort of betrayal or expulsion.

Children who unconsciously expect acts of violence (this will be seen to apply not only to Cordelia but also to Kent and to Lear himself) quite often feel compelled to disobey in order to be punished, since however severe such punishment may be it is reassuring compared to the sword of Damocles they always expect a cruel parent to let fall on their heads. If this is true in the present context, Cordelia's behavior toward her father might be prompted by a consideration such as: you cannot reject me (and even placing me on the same level as my sisters is tantamount to rejection) for *I* shall leave *you* by forcing you to send me away.[20]

As happens when violent and unexpected disappointments occur, Cordelia is transformed from the apple of Lear's eye into a distressing nightmare. The Fool appears on the scene when Cordelia leaves and, by contrast, disappears forever when she returns. Giorgio Strehler, who gave both the part of Cordelia and that of the Fool to the Italian actress Ottavia Piccolo, must have sensed the mysterious link between the two characters.[21] Moreover, the two are confused even in Lear's mind. Of the dead Cordelia he says: "And my poor fool is hanged! No, no, no life" (5.3.281). This connection between Cordelia and the Fool cannot be explained only on practical historical grounds, such as the small number of boy actors in the Elizabethan and Jacobean theater companies.

Unexpectedly, and therefore traumatically, Cordelia stops acting as a support to her father's weak self-esteem, and Lear finds himself totally unprepared to meet the crisis of being unable to control events, as his rank had always led him to believe he could. He is suddenly brought face to face with his own smallness and his mad fear of disintegration and compensates by turning himself into an omnipotent dragon, invoker of lightning and hurler of maledictions. He is in fact nothing but an anxiety-ridden child, which is underlined by the fact that no one is affected by his rage—neither his daughters nor even Kent. Imagining that he is a raging dragon is of use to nobody but himself.[22]

Although nineteenth-century criticism ascribed Cordelia's pride to her uprightness, it springs from something different: it is the characteristic of the hero who indulges in excessive defense— Cordelia is a sort of Saint George.[23] Throughout the first scene, indeed, the myth of England's patron saint forms a background to events. Even Kent half assumes the tones of a Saint George cast in the same mold and comes between the dragon and the damsel in distress. Lear warns him:

Peace, Kent.
Come not between the dragon and his wrath. (1.1.121–22)

From this moment on, the king's enfeebled mind begins to wander.

Cordelia's apparent indifference to her father's kingdom probably conceals a more complex situation. If it is true that she needs to have all of her father's love, to the exclusion of her sisters, might not her total need also extend to his kingdom, which has become a symbol of his love? It is not by chance that she marries France and brings England's traditional enemy across the waters to attempt to conquer the whole kingdom, not just her part of it.

Have such suggestions aroused indignation in Cordelia's many admirers? On the other hand, does seeing Cordelia as venerably maternal, as Victor Hugo does,[24] enhance the humanity of this extraordinary character? In order to understand her devastating tragic conflict, it would perhaps be opportune to consider the words that come to her spontaneously as she waits to meet with the English army marching against her. They could not be more revealing:

No blown ambition doth our arms incite,
But love, dear love, and our aged father's right. (4.3.27–28)

They are in fact the crucial key to a full understanding of this character. Her statement is a *Verneinung*, a negation that reveals the very desire that it seeks to conceal and disown.[25] The question Freud might have asked in order to understand the defensive function of *negation* in this case would have been more or less: What actually suggests to Cordelia that she is spurred on by ambition if not an unknown voice that comes from within? This mechanism was, of course, already familiar in the days of the classical dictum *excusatio non petita accusatio manifesta*, which was dear to both Terence and Saint Augustine. Without realizing it, Cordelia admits that "blown ambition" *has* led her to take up arms.

On the battlefield, the shadow of death hangs over her and her hated sisters: it is the final clash. Her mind cannot but be shaken; long-standing family conflicts must be newly awakened. Whenever we are excited, perturbed, or impatient, our self-control is weakened and the true nature of our thoughts and desires is revealed in what we say. To quote the words of Cordelia herself: "ungoverned rage [may] dissolve the life / That wants the means to lead it" (4.3.19–20).[26]

In any case, with her unexpected refusal to enter the competition, Cordelia turns into a wicked mother in Lear's eyes. A terrible, primitive mother who denies him her understanding. It is now time to return to the Fool and to the king's madness.

The Fool and Melancholy

A marginal comment about the figure of the Fool needs to be made. In Shakespeare's plays there are "clownish servants," such as Speed in *The Two Gentlemen of Verona*, the clown in *Measure for Measure,* the two clowns in *Hamlet,* Feste, who is a combination of the witty fool and the gay minstrel, Lancelot Gobbo in *The Merchant of Venice,* and Touchstone in *As You Like It,* yet the Fool in *Lear* is the only real *fool.* It might be objected that all such characters are fools, but I shall attempt to defend my hypothesis with further evidence. The figure of the fool and his derivatives, from the buffoon to Pierrot and numerous later clowns, has fascinated a number of critics and scholars. Enid Welsford, for example, has traced their social and literary history,[27] and Mikhail Bakhtin has detected in both the figure of the *fol* and the *sot* the king of an "upside down world," where "praise and insult merge indissolubly."[28]

Vanna Gentili implicitly criticizes those who favor indiscriminate classifications. Because of the fool's multifarious ancestors, she acknowledges that he is a composite figure "who embodies the coexistence of antinomian terms, in addition to expressing a philosophy that reconciles opposites and a morality aimed at resolving contradictions in the name of the common sense usually associated with the unsophisticated," which, she perceptively underlines, "shows an acceptance of appearances or, better still, a medieval faith in the certainty that follows." She does not, however, indulge in excessive generalizations; she is aware that Lear's Fool represents an exception in the category of the "two-faced fool," with his "threefold personality—at times innocent and generous, at other times astute and malicious." He is an exception because of a peculiarity not shared by his predecessors: perspicacious innocence is replaced by the cynicism of an acrimonious censor.[29]

Tolstoy displayed a singular hatred of Shakespeare, who had always caused him "unbearable repulsion and tedium," and made an analysis of *Lear* that was as meticulous as it was arbitrary, in an effort to prove that Shakespeare not only possessed no genius but was not even a "writer of average talent." With a perspicacity he did not always show, anarchic Orwell sensed that what Tolstoy wished to destroy in Shakespeare-Lear were those aspects of himself that he refused to accept, especially his increasingly repressive authoritarianism during the last few years of his life.[30]

This observation bears a strong resemblance to what was earlier hypothesized about the relationship between Gustave Flaubert and Charbovari.

It is interesting to observe the great Russian writer's approach to the Fool, who represents Lear's madness and, according to Orwell, the mad part of Tolstoy himself. Tolstoy had well-defined tastes: he clearly preferred the happy ending of *King Leir* (one of Shakespeare's sources), a play that "ends in a more natural manner, which accords with the moral expectations of the audience, unlike Shakespeare's [play]; above all the King of the Gauls defeats the elder sisters' husbands and Cordelia, instead of being killed, restores Lear to the throne." He considers the storm "unnecessary" and the Fool a "mere nuisance," an excuse for introducing humor in bad taste. Such a drastic pronouncement about the Fool suggests that it is this character which disturbs him most.[31]

The history of the criticism and staging of *King Lear* shows that the Fool has also caused sharp division and radical reactions in figures less representative than Tolstoy: some are enthralled by the Fool, others want to eliminate him. This is because he is emblematic of a well-defined psychic presence. Charles A. Brown, one of his most fervent admirers, rhapsodizes as follows in his *Shakespeare's Autobiographical Poems* of 1838:

Now, our joy, though last, not least, my dearest of all Fools, Lear's Fool! Ah, what a noble heart, a gentle and loving one, lies beneath that parti-coloured jerkin! Thou hast been cruelly treated. Regan and Goneril could but hang thee.[32] . . . But let me take thee, without addition and diminution, from the hands of Sh., and then art thou one of his most perfect creations. Look at him! It may be your eyes see him not as mine do, but he appears to me of a light, delicate frame, every feature expressive of sensitivity, even to pain, with eyes lustrously intelligent, a mouth blandly beautiful, and withal a hectic flush upon his cheek. Oh that I were a painter![33]

In justification of his appraisal, he asks sorrowfully: "When Lear is in the storm, who is with him? None,—not even Kent.—None but the Fool; who labours to outjest His heart-struck injuries."[34] This construction can, however, easily be dismantled: So long as the Fool is present in the storm scene, Lear continues to talk about "filial ingratitude" (3.4.14). Only when the Fool has left does he utter the invocation that is a sign of his great personal crisis. Brown's opinion was widely accepted and held ground through to our own times.

Some years ago, Robert H. Goldsmith, author of *Wise Fools in Shakespeare*, wrote that when the Fool abandons all caution to follow his sick master, he is the embodiment of the Christian doctrine of wise madness.[35] Around the time when Brown was writing his unreserved panegyrics, the great actor William Macready (he had in a sense taken the place of Edmund Kean, who had died less than five years earlier) noted in his diary:

(4 January 1838): Went to the theatre, where I went on a first rehearsal of *King Lear*. My opinion of the introduction of the Fool is that, like many such terrible contrasts in poetry and painting, in acting-representation it will fail of effect; it will either weary and annoy or distract the spectator. I have no hope of it, and think that at the last we shall be obliged to dispense with it.[36]

Brown's own words show that the Fool played a part in his adolescence: "Oh that I could describe him as I knew him in my boyhood, when the Fool made me shed tears, while Lear did but terrify me!"[37] William Macready's diary tells us that he changed his mind on the following day. He had already decided to do away with that character when "Bartley observed that a woman should play it. I caught at the idea, and instantly exclaimed, 'Miss P. Horton is the very person!' I was delighted at the thought."[38] The extremely well-informed Marvin Rosenberg reports that in the end Macready staged *Lear* with the Fool in it, as well as much of the original Shakespearean text.[39] On that occasion Macready sought (not with complete success according to the critics) to reconstruct the image of a *strong* Lear.

It seems superfluous to say that Brown idealized the Fool. I happen to be in total agreement with those who believe the Fool to be a great Shakespearean creation (and I shall try to demonstrate this) but why Brown should have been moved to tears in his adolescence by the words of the Fool has yet to be explained. The emphasis, the affectionate outburst that Brown reserves for the Fool give the impression of being propitiatory, suggesting that in his unconscious he might be *afraid* of this most beautiful of beings, who is all goodness and splendor. After all, the words "it may be your eyes see him not as mine do" appear to offer an unintentional glimpse of his own doubt. His notes seem to suggest that his idealization of the Fool served to counterbalance the presence of a terrifying father. Macready, by contrast, suddenly changed his mind about cutting this difficult character when he realized he could assign the part *to a woman:* yet beside the Fool he was to construct a particularly robust Lear—a fact that may not be altogether unrelated.

In 1940, John Gielgud made his Fool the externalization of Lear's need to punish himself: Gielgud's Lear used the whip but the Fool also whipped Lear. The Hungarian actor Gyorgy Kalman offered a similar interpretation in the seventies. With felicitous insight Lloyd Hoff's design for the cover of Rosenberg's book, *The Masks of King Lear,* showed a Janus with the face of a desperate king on the right and a sneering Fool on the left. "The Fool and Lear are an indivisible equation," comments Rosenberg, "which has a third, implicit term in it: Cordelia."[40] As a materialization of Lear's need for self-punishment, the Fool is felt by some to be one of the dramatis personae who inhabit the king's interior world, just like the "false justicer" of the third act.

Within a more "naturalistic" framework, and bearing in mind that fools characteristically adapt their behavior to suit the figure to which they are assigned, another hypothesis might be suggested: Lear's Fool acts at the prompting of the old king's projective identifications.[41]

Many instances of psychic repression result from internal dictatorships.[42] These dictators tend to sacrifice to the domain of Narcissus (where the need of fellow human beings has no place) those parts of the individual which, prompted by Eros, would prefer to have good relationships with others, sensing that this is the only way toward self-fulfillment. These healthy parts become capable of loving in a mature sense only if they manage to overcome both their own closedness and their narcissistic tendency to exploit others (as has been seen in Lear). Taoists see these as the good qualities of the Tao, which human beings must adopt as a model to be followed; for Buddhists they are the internal Buddha; Socrates calls them the daemon, while for Christians they are the imitation of Christ. Obviously everyone has his own idea of mature love. Taking care of these parts, however, goes hand in hand with caring for others. It is what Lear is trying to achieve and the Fool is trying to *prevent* by all possible means.

To think that the Fool "labours to out-jest [Lear's] heart-struck injuries" (3.1.7–8), as the Gentleman does, means not having very clear ideas on the subject. By using the technique of speaking nonsense, the Fool strikes at the king's heart and paralyzes him. All of his sayings and jokes revolve around one single piece of advice: Why do you need your daughters' love, Lear? You ought to worry about your own crown! The proverbial language used by the Fool is concerned with self-protection and property rights.

The part that needs to give and receive love is quite often symbolized by a woman or a child. In *Doctor Faustus*, Thomas Mann describes the atrocious death of a child, which seals the pact between the devil and Leverkuhn; the black masses celebrated by Voisin the witch and Guibourg the abbot involved cutting the throats of children. These are the defenseless, vulnerable, naked beings whom Lear learns to accept as he cries out in the storm—once he is free of the Fool, who is the great enemy of the needy child:

> Poor naked wretches, wheresoe'er you are,
> That bide the pelting of this pitiless storm,
> How shall your houseless heads and unfed sides,
> Your looped and windowed raggedness, defend you
> From seasons such as these? (3.4.28–32)

The Fool's Techniques

The Fool represents the sadistic and perverse voice of Lear, a voice that attacks all bonds in order to forestall being abandoned.

Having been betrayed in his earliest infancy, Lear does not want to repeat the experience. Thus, subtly, often seductively, using confusion and maneuvers that Gregory Bateson calls "double bind,"[43] he castrates every impulse, every manifestation of disinterested affection. It is as well to point out that saboteurs like the Fool are often the most cunning and dialectically most capable parts of a human being. "He is as cunning as the devil," says an old adage. Careful observation will clearly reveal that the Fool, like any able dictator, does not give explanations but expresses himself in maxims that, though they are largely indecipherable, have enormous suggestive power. He offers interpretations of the present that sound obvious only because he has abstracted the present from the past; in this sense he is the standard-bearer of confusion disguised as wisdom. The Fool mocks and subdues the king, makes him feel foolish and inadequate. Lear does not want to be derided or taunted, and yet he helps the Fool to deride and taunt him.

At one point Lear says that he has had to dismiss fifty knights from his retinue, though Goneril had not mentioned a precise number. This instance is quoted by Andrew C. Bradley as one of the play's baffling inconsistencies. Kenneth Muir comments (ironically one hopes) that Lear was perhaps endowed with telepathic power.[44] It might be suggested, however, that this is an explicit sign that Lear is moved by unconscious feelings of guilt, by a desire to curb both his sadism and disintegrative power.

A further sign is to be found in act 1, scene 4, where Lear shows concern for his eldest daughter's problems. He knows that his men are quarrelsome and insolent to her, and he betrays a hint of anxiety:

How now, daughter? What makes that frontlet on?
You are too much of late i' th' frown. (1.4.171–72)

But the Fool does not look kindly on this sort of feeling, he likes strong men who make no mistakes. Concern for others is a sign of weakness. His is a philosophy that might be called phallic.[45] What does the Fool say, then, to prevent him from taking this dangerous direction?

Thou wast a pretty fellow when thou hadst no need
to care for her frowning; now thou art an O without
a figure. I am better than thou art, now. I am a Fool;
thou art nothing. (1.4.173–76)

It is as if he were saying, A father who worries about his daughter's frown does not deserve to exist. Let us look more closely at
the text. The Fool says, You were a pretty fellow (i.e., healthy,
strong) when you did not bother yourself about your daughter's
frown. Here the Fool denies that Lear is tormented out of genuine concern and insinuates with the words "no need to care" that
Lear worries solely because he is enfeebled, because he has to
study the expression of a woman who has become his ruler for
signs of fair or foul weather. This is a cynical, perverse attack that
makes negative something that is at most ambivalent. Furthermore, what does he remind him of? "Thou art nothing," that
same tragic *nothing* that Cordelia had flung in his face.

A little later on, the Fool comments on Goneril's attempt to
make her father see reason and suggests to Lear that he is like the
stupid sparrow who rears a cuckoo:

. . . The hedge-sparrow fed the cuckoo so long,
That it's had it head bit off by it young. . . . (1.4.198–99)

It is as if he were saying: Why try to reason? She is not your flesh
and blood, she wants to devour you! Lear does not disown her
but vacillates and asks: "Are you our daughter?" (1.4.201).

From another point of view, the relationship between Lear and
the Fool defines the area where different worldviews come into
violent collision and drive the king to madness. It will later be
shown that this passage contains the idea (though it is only barely
hinted at) that Goneril and Regan are not cuckoos but Lear's
own flesh and blood, grown from his own seed. At the same time,
there is the opposite idea, dictated by a paranoid drive to power
(as Elias Canetti developed the concept),[46] which desires to protect the king according to the cynical logic of *homo homini lupus*.

As Hegel perceived, despotism and the rise to power at all costs
demand drastic sacrifices—both internally and socially—of the

person who imposes them. Shakespeare makes Lady Macbeth an archetype of such violence:

> . . . I have given suck, and know
> How tender 'tis to love the babe that milks me.
> I would, while it was smiling in my face,
> Have plucked my nipple from his boneless gums,
> And dashed the brains out, had I so sworn
> As you have done to this.[47]

The Coxcomb

The Phallus towers over two myths: the myth of fertility and that of uncontested sadistic dominion. The Fool makes his entrance offering his coxcomb to the Earl of Kent. Is this mere chance? The coxcomb is an obvious phallic symbol, at least as obvious as the bauble, the Fool's obscenely shaped stick.[48] A phallus was mounted on the poles of Greek phallophori, and enormous phalluses were also worn by Doric mimes.

The custom of keeping dwarfs or mentally disturbed people ("natural fools") in a family household can be dated back to Roman times, when well-to-do families kept hideous imbeciles as if they were pets, just as ladies later kept monkeys (Sarah Bernhardt is said to have had one). In his eighth epigram, Martial says that these mentally retarded creatures were sold in the monster markets, and the madder they were the more they cost. The custom of keeping fools as jesters grew in the Middle Ages. Such deformed or mentally deficient beings belonged to the households of kings, noblemen, and even high-ranking churchmen. From a psycho-sociological point of view, this might be seen as a *caste* phenomenon, an attempt to exorcise either madness or the feelings of guilt about occupying a privileged position—an early model for marginalization in order to exercise apparent control over what is "different" as well as over aspects of oneself that one wishes to alienate or disown. This might explain why a sensitive man like Thomas More kept Patteson, his own domestic fool. The possibility of indulging in licentious talk with impunity, of uttering forbidden "truths," of parodying the master's faults and weaknesses must have provided a fairly strong incentive for perfectly sane social outcasts to join the ranks of the artificial fools.

Rosenberg, who has dissected *King Lear* more fully than most, points out that we know a few things about the Fool even before seeing him. Lear needs his Fool, is dependent on him, misses him, and the Fool is pining for Cordelia.

It was suggested earlier that the Fool attacks Lear's relationships of affective dependence; he sees himself as the king's sole adviser and is deeply attached to the daughter who has rebelled and created the "empty space" in Lear. The Fool makes his entrance during the fourth scene of act 1, where a speech by Kent is followed by Lear's peremptory words "Let me not stay a jot for dinner" (1.4.8).[49] Lear undoubtedly needs to assert his authority yet again; at the same time no words could have better expressed the king's greed.

That melancholy is connected with voracity (or "orality conflicts," as psychoanalysis has called it since Karl Abraham) has been known for centuries. Robert Burton pointed it out about fifteen years after the first performance of *King Lear*.[50] In a short chapter toward the end of *The Anatomy of Melancholy*, Burton describes the relationship of an infant with its nurse as one of the first possible causes of melancholy: "From a child's nativity, the first ill accident that can likely befall him . . . is a bad nurse, by whose means alone he may be tainted with this malady from his cradle."[51]

Burton points out that Favorinus goes even further, showing that "if a nurse be mis-shapen, unchaste, unhonest, impudent, drunk, cruel and the like, the child that sucks upon her breast will be so too; all other affections of the mind and diseases are almost ingrafted, as it were, and imprinted into the temperature of the infant by the nurse's milk." Even Caligula's cruelty is attributed to a cruel nurse: "*Et si delira fuerit, infantulum delirum faciet:* if she be a fool or dolt, the child she nurseth will take after her."[52] Burton's reference in the same work to a passage taken from a

Latin treatise bears a striking resemblance to Lear's invocation during the storm and his attempts at expiation. As a cure for melancholy, Guainerius advised one patient to wear a hair shirt next to his skin, to go barefoot in cold weather, and to whip himself now and then as monks do, but above all, to fast.[53] Fasting, then, is thought to be a general, sufficient remedy.

Burton classifies the relationship of the infant with a nurse and her milk among the "non-necessary, remote, outward, adventitious or accidental" causes of melancholy; psychoanalysts of recent generations maintain that the problem has its origins in the infant's earliest losses—birth and weaning.[54]

A comparison between melancholy and mourning is still probably the best way to summarize what occurs. Both cases involve loss, abandonment. What is lost in mourning is a real, consciously perceived person, while the melancholy person is not aware of loss (Lear is not aware of feeling desperate because Cordelia has abandoned him). At their root is an unresolved ambivalence comprising love and hate, request and refusal. In order to stop suffering, the subject attempts to deny all distance: the person who is abandoned becomes one with the abandoner and, like a cannibal, devours him or her; but in this way resentment and rage are internalized.[55]

The greedier the individual who seeks to overcome melancholy, the more he feels unconsciously powerless to repair what he has despoiled in his greedy fantasies. His efforts to recognize not only the needy, infantile parts of himself but also his devastating guilt are bound to fail and thus he will feel obliged to direct his accusations at others:

> . . . Tremble, thou wretch,
> That hast within thee undivulgèd crimes,
> Unwhipped of justice; hide thee, thou bloody hand,
> Thou perjured, and thou simular of virtue
> That art incestuous; caitiff, to pieces shake,
> That under covert and convenient seeming
> Has practised on man's life; close pent-up guilts
> Rive your concealing continents and cry

These dreadful summoners grace. I am a man
More sinned against than sinning. (3.2.51–60)

Unable to keep the wretched parts of himself internalized, Lear
is forced to project them. This is his real tragedy. What he describes in the recondite, ineluctably rejected image is himself. He
will never discover that the perjurer, the committer of incest, the
bloodthirsty creature he speaks of are all inside him: a pitiless
Fool forbids him "the awful daring of a moment's surrender" and
relegates him forever to the role of victim, thus preventing him
from taking care of the needy parts of himself. With his assertion
"I am a man / more sinn'd against than sinning," the king seals
his unfair account of events.

In the light of this analysis, *King Lear* unfolds as the chronicle
of an attempt to overcome tremendous remorse. It would also be
possible to reread the figure of Lear by seeking the less conspic-
uous signs of his unconscious feelings of guilt. For example, when
Kent berates the king at the beginning of the play for his behavior
toward Cordelia, Lear does not tell him he, Kent, is wrong or
repeat his own harsh accusations against his daughter. Instead, he
diverts Kent's attention, reproaching him for having dared to tell
the king to break his sacred vow. He twice justifies his behavior:
"to break our vows? . . . we durst never yet!" The request to sus-
pend the sentence pronounced against Cordelia is an act of pre-
sumption that "nor our nature nor our place can bear" (1.1.167–68;
170). He evokes honor in order to avoid the pangs of guilt.

Although Lear's anguish reaches its peak during the storm, the
result will be equally tragic. He admits his guilt and his insensitivity toward Cordelia, but he projects them immediately onto
others: "Oh, you are men of stones!" (5.3.232).[56] He repeats himself. He is forced to: it is the others, not he, who are made of
stone! Above all, however, Lear's efforts fail because he sees
Goneril and Regan, the little girls to whom he has been unable to
give enough love, as enemies to the very end. He seems to feel
more devastating remorse toward Regan, for Goneril had sought
conflict (1.3.13–22). Lear's mock trial of his daughters is the most
moving evidence of the laceration that divides the king between

his need to continue to blame and his profound wish to absolve them by making himself the object of accusation. Not everyone is able to contain this awful laceration, not even the spectator. The absence of the entire trial scene from the Folio text of *Lear* is perhaps a sign that it was unsuccessful in Shakespeare's time.

The storm is now over. The king has gained painful insight into many things, but the need to deny is still tremendously present. The Fool's final enigmatic inquiry ("tell me whether a madman be a gentleman or a yeoman") has heated the old father's scepter again:

> . . . To have a thousand
> with red burning spits come hissing in upon them! (Q13.11–12)

The sort of arraignment he stages, aided by Kent and the Fool, with Edgar in contrast, is no mock trial as has been assumed; it is a delirious representation of what is seething in the depths of his own soul:

> Arraign her first; 'tis Goneril. I here take my oath
> before this honourable assembly, she kicked the
> poor King her father.
>
> . . . .
>
> And here's another, whose warp'd looks proclaim
> What store her heart is made on. Stop her there!
> Arms, arms, sword, fire! Corruption in the place!
> False justicer, why hast thou let her 'scape? (Q13.42–51)

Where does the hallucinated image erupt from if not out of his heart? Who could be the false judge that allows the accused to escape if not some part of himself that feels like a failed and desperate father? Lear later wonders "which is the justicer, which is the thief?" (4.4.149–50). The question earns him Edgar's blessing. The Fool will not pronounce another word except to announce his final exit. The hounds of remorse, the entire pack, have caught up with the father, who has tired of struggling:

> The little dogs and all,
> Tray, Blanch and Sweetheart—see, they bark at me. (3.6.21–22)

To those who wonder whether the ending of *King Lear* suggests redemption or disintegration, it can be suggested that Lear reaches only the threshold of redemption, if redemption is understood as freedom from the paralyzing grip of guilt. In his own way, he comes to terms with this freedom but only in relation to Cordelia. The king avoids disintegration but never finds the strength to accept the terrible accusations that, albeit unconsciously, he levels at himself. And this prevents him from overcoming them.[57]

It is, of course, true that he manages to say, "None does offend, I say none; I'll able 'em" (4.5.164), but his paranoid rage immediately explodes again against his daughters and sons-in-law:

> . . . And when I have stolen upon these son-in-laws,
> then kill, kill, kill, kill, kill, kill. (4.5.182–83)

The Barbarous Scythian

On being rejected by Cordelia, experienced as mother, the breast that abandons him, Lear is panic-stricken:

> . . . For, by the sacred radiance of the sun,
> The mysteries of Hecate and the night,
> By all the operations of the orbs
> From whom we do exist and cease to be,
> Here I disclaim all my paternal care,
> Propinquity and property of blood,
> And as a stranger to my heart and me
> Hold thee from this forever. The barbarous Scythian,
> Or he that makes his generation messes
> To gorge his appetite, shall to my bosom,
> Be as well neighboured, pitied, and relieved
> As thou, my sometime daughter. (1.1.109–20)

In *Macbeth*, Hecate is described as the queen of witches. Already invoked in pre-Hellenistic fertility rites, she is a fundamentally matriarchal figure, the demonic side of phallic Artemis. There are allusions to her as maiden and mother in more than one of Shakespeare's plays. Emanating from darkness, she appears uttering excommunications and armed with poisons and daggers, demanding sacrificial offerings.[58] The witch, the queen of the night, is the evil mother, the mother who does not give herself, and is also made spiteful by the fury projected onto her by the neglected child, rendered voracious by his raging hunger.[59]

With her unexpected "Nothing," Cordelia lacerates the mouth of the child-Lear with the same violence as the "plucked nipple" of Lady Macbeth. Immediately afterward the king alternates between the holy radiance of the sun (perhaps the mother's face confused with the good breast that gives warmth and light to the infant-earth) and the night, which implies absence of the sun and presence of the queen of the night, Hecate. He is aware that the "operation of the orbs" is involved. But what are the first spheres each of us needed when we came into the world? Breasts are of central importance to the whole scene: Lear expected "nursery" from Cordelia, but it is to the much "professed bosom" of the rival sisters that an enraged Cordelia leaves her father. Hecate is the breast that refuses sustenance. For this reason she is related to the phantoms of Hades: without an adequate breast the infant perishes.

When weaning is abrupt, feelings of persecution reach a peak. For the desperate infant howling inside Lear, too, the relationship with the breast is a matter of life and death ("the orbs / From whom we do exist and cease to be"). All dependence must therefore be hurriedly canceled, and Lear believes he can magically find safety by denying the blood relationship with his daughter-mother: if there is no bond with Cordelia, the chasms will not open. He also disowns Goneril, turning her into a "degenerate bastard" (1.4.232).

But even all this is not sufficient to placate his despair, to reduce the "empty space" that has invaded him. In these desperate situations we devour those who have abandoned us so as to become one with them. Once he has turned into the barbarous Scythian who makes food of his children, Lear enacts his identification with the lost breast through a rhetorical figure ("they shall to my bosom . . . be relieved") so that he can become the one who has abandoned and thus deny that he has been left.

Later Lear will give a perfect description of himself as an omnipotent child, although he accuses Goneril and Regan of having made him such—as if these two daughters had been born before him and were his mothers:

> They flattered me
> like a dog and told me I had the white hairs in my
> beard ere the black ones were there. To say "ay" and
> "no" to everything that I said "ay" and "no" to was no
> good divinity. When the rain came to wet me once,
> and the wind to make me chatter; when the thunder
> would not peace at my bidding, there I found 'em,
> there I smelt 'em out. Go to, they are not men o' their
> words. They told me I was everything; 'tis a lie, I am
> not ague-proof. (4.5.96–105)[60]

The Egg and the Two Crowns

Before suggesting a possible interpretation of one of the Fool's famous provocations, I am obliged to open another, not particularly simple parenthesis. The minds of those who go through the storm of melancholy are filled with fantasies representing the first two dramatic (sometimes tragic) separations in every human life: birth and weaning from a nurturing breast. I have already mentioned this, but it is worth repeating. The banishment from the garden of Eden is a prime example of the fusion of these fantasies into one metaphor.[61] At the peak of depressive suffering, this process of merging is accompanied by what Donald Meltzer calls "zonal confusion," a somewhat dry expression meaning that certain areas of the body, together with their products and contents, are mentally confused with each other, almost as if they meant the same thing.[62]

A further reference to *vox populi* will help to introduce this disconcerting phenomenon: certain corruptions of colorful everyday speech are unmistakably products of the unconscious. Before the word "ass" is considered, it would be as well to mention that in Castillian iconoclastic parlance, the word "leche" (milk) is used disparagingly to mean "sperm," while in Italy expressions such as "faccia di culo" (literally, arse-face) and "testa di cazzo" (cock-head) suggest an analogous phenomenon of contamination and confusion. The mouth that needs the nipple, the symbol of the infant's need, is often confused with another orifice, the anus, which, by appropriating the omnipotent phallus, exercises *captatio penis*. This is the perverse overturning of the master-servant relationship: the servant captures and dominates the former master.[63]

The ideal omnipotent situation is that of an Eden evoked by our own nostalgia. In the fusion that occurs inside the womb, the infant is one with the mother's body. In this fantasy, need is denied: there is no separation, no lack, and the fetus is the lord of creation. The praise and the tributes of subjection that Lear clearly needs to such an inordinate extent represent a palliative to deny that the illusion of Eden is no longer possible. Lear's realization of the loss of this omnipotence is painfully registered in the words "they told me I was everything" (4.5.104).

When the king decides to give his property to his daughters and to this end opens a contest for succession, he is begging for adulation and therefore openly showing his own need. He tries to keep all dangerous aspects under control and, above all, dominate one particular obsession: the terror of possibly being abandoned by those he needs as a result of his greedy, despotic demands. With his hundred knights he hopes to control the nipple-phalluses, the daughters to whom he has given away both scepter and armies.

The tragedy of poor Lear seems to rest on the simplest of truths: he organizes a love contest because he cannot imagine being loved simply as a parent who has given enough of what normally causes children to be grateful. In reality he has given affection (otherwise many of his daughters' reactions would be incomprehensible), yet he does not seem to be deeply aware of this. He strips himself of his kingdom as if he wished to barter it for love. When parents do not have this sort of conviction, they behave in an authoritarian manner and try to obtain signs of affection with more or less controlled violence. Cordelia, however, breaks the spell of absolute dominion and a devastating void opens up, a void that is devastating also because he then loses control over his other two daughters.

So much for this lengthy digression. Let us now consider the Fool's provocation and the manner in which he torments Lear:

Fool　. . . Nuncle, give me an egg, and I'll give thee two crowns.

Lear　What two crowns shall they be?

Fool　Why, after I have cut the egg i' th' middle and eat
　　　　up the meat, the two crowns of the egg. When thou
　　　　clovest thy crown i' th' middle, and gavest away both
　　　　parts, thou borest thine ass o' th' back o'er the dirt. (1.4.138–43)

In his final remark, the Fool is alluding to a fable, possibly by Aesop, about a man, his two sons, and the ass. According to William Warner, the source for this is to be found in *Albion's England* (1586). But this particular interpretation does not take into account further connotations of the word "ass," which means not only *equus asinus* but also, in American slang, "buttocks" or "rectum" and (in rare, mainly regional cases) "woman."[64]

Thus, the Fool is making fun of Lear by more or less saying, If you break the splendid symbiosis (a child in the mother's womb) that is an egg and, like the barbarous Scythian, devour its contents (Shakespeare uses the word "meat"), you will reveal your own deep need to be nourished. The egg is an appropriate symbol of independent nourishment because it is able to contain both the fetus and its needs. In this way the Fool shows Lear the anxieties connected with separation from the womb.

The empty womb symbolized by an open shell, a cave, or other concave, uterine objects emerges in the conscious or unconscious fantasies in the critical moments that evoke birth. An egg also hangs motionless above the head of the Virgin Mother and the Christ Child in the altarpiece painted at Urbino by Piero della

Francesca and now part of the permanent collection in the Pinacoteca di Brera in Milan.

When Lear abdicates his role as sovereign—a totally independent figure, at once mother and child—he leaves the paradise of intrauterine life, where every organ of the mother's body, like every subject in the kingdom, is at his beck and call ("Let me not stay a jot for dinner"). When the spell is broken and he deliberately renounces Eden, he moves into a world where needs may not be fulfilled, where it is no longer possible to deny the need of the essential "other" that we have all been dependent upon—the mother's body.

If for one reason or another this need is extreme, the infant experiences birth as a threat and the shell becomes a matrix of persecution, a symbol of expulsion and rejection. It is with this very shell that Lear crowns his daughters, which prompts the Fool basically to say: You wanted to renounce the paradise of your omnipotence? What an ass you have been! Now you are carrying your anus on your back, above your shit. Now your dependent part, which you should have concealed from the world, is degraded (because it is dirty).

As if this were not explicit enough, he adds: You wanted to show your dependence? Well, now they've stuck it up your ass.

Lear When were you wont to be so full of songs, sirrah?
Fool I have used it, nuncle, e'er since thou madest thy
daughters thy mothers, for when thou gavest them the
rod and puttest down thy breeches,

> Then they for sudden joy did weep,
> And I for sorrow sung,
> That such a king should play bo-peep
> And go the fools among. (1.4.152–59)

The violence of the Fool's phallic logic seems to become clearer here: Since you turned your daughters into mothers, you have given them the phallus-scepter and have offered them your buttocks (you have let down your breeches). To show oneself dependent, needy, childish ("play bo-beep") is pure folly according to the Fool's phallic logic.

Noble Kent

Kent is surely another character deprived of adequate dramatic dignity by traditional criticism. He is undoubtedly brave, and his defense of Cordelia shows that he is not small-minded. It is as well to bear in mind such qualities. Lear had dismissed his daughter with the words "Let pride, which she calls plainness, marry her" (1.1.129). Rising to her defense, Kent strikes home with noble words and takes up the theme of the ability to be "true and plain."

> To plainness honour's bound
> When majesty falls to folly. . . . (1.1.148–49)

But as soon as one dares to remove the cultural bell jar under which such plainness has been preserved, it turns out to be something quite complex, just like the young princess's feelings.

To begin with, one of Kent's undoubted limitations is his inability to perceive that beneath Lear's blindness and injustice, beneath his insensitivity, lies madness. His inner tensions are near breaking point and about to explode. It would be unfair, however, to reproach Kent for this lack of "diagnostic" skill. This type of clinical sensitivity, presupposing as it does a detachment that is certainly not easy to achieve, would only gradually be constructed and modified over the course of centuries and acquire proper theorization in the second half of the twentieth century. As it is, none of the characters is able to comprehend the king's serious pathology. Goneril speaks of simple "dotage" when referring to her father's condition (1.4.306). With the exception of what happens at the climax of the tragedy, when Lear is called "mad" it is in a rhetorical rather than a clinical sense. Kent sees that the king "falls to folly" and denounces him for it, but his words seem to mean that Lear is foolishly unfair (one wonders why Kent did not find the love contest equally foolish). This, then, is not a fruitful point of departure for understanding the text.

In the opening scene, after shouting at Lear, who is in the process of disinheriting Cordelia, "whilst I can vent clamour from my throat, / I'll tell thee thou dost evil" (1.1.164–65), and having more or less accused him of being a tyrant,

> Fare thee well, King; sith thus thou wilt appear,
> Freedom lives hence, and banishment is here (1.1.179–80),[65]

what does Kent then do? He leaves the court and subsequently behaves in a way that flatly contradicts his "plainness": he humbles himself, adopts a disguise (also obviously to save his life), and *lies.* At first sight, this behavior does not tally with the traditional image of Kent (one that he continues to reinforce), the image of a rough champion of truth at all costs. And he lies in a rather servile, obsequious manner.

Lear What art thou?
Kent A very honest-hearted fellow, and as poor as the
        King.
Lear If thou be'st as poor for a subject as he's for a King,
        thou 'rt poor enough. What wouldst thou?
Kent Service.
Lear Who wouldst thou serve?
Kent You.
Lear Dost thou know me, fellow?
Kent No, sir; but you have that in your countenance
        which I would fain call master.
Lear What's that?
Kent Authority. (1.4.18–30)

It is difficult to agree with anyone who maintains that this is essentially a portrait of filial love, devoted friendship, or loyalty of a subject to his king. Just like Goneril (and Regan), Kent shows himself to be well aware of the drug Lear needs, of the words he wants to hear to lift his morale: you are not an evil tyrant but a man gifted with authority. And since "authority" derives from *auctor,* meaning one who originates, generates, it is as if Kent were reassuring Lear by alluding to the fact that he is a good father and worthy of being served. Leaving aside this (somewhat forced) etymological digression, there still seems to be little doubt that Kent has totally changed his approach at this point.

But the question is, why should he do this? Let us assume that he does it out of a spirit of altruism, that he is spurred on by a wish to help the old king—by what might in modern terms be defined as a sort of confused but sincere psychotherapeutic impulse. Let us assume that he does this because (contrary to my own hypothesis) he has understood that Lear is on the brink of insanity. In this case Kent is an inept carer.

When berating the king before his court and then flattering him when there is no audience, Kent undoubtedly adopts discordant attitudes—inappropriately in both cases. On the first occasion, he speaks as the voice of responsible reason when Lear, who is thrown off balance by Cordelia's unexpected "Nothing" and suffers an anxiety crisis, loses his reason and is therefore in need of soothing words, inviting breasts, and calming milk. Critical unawareness of the desperate child inside a ranting king has meant that the latent meaning of Kent's lines has always been distorted. When considered objectively, Kent's reasonableness is seen to be an attack by a bully who rises to the enemy's defense when Lear feels that he has received a mortal blow. Indeed, what word does Shakespeare significantly have the king pronounce? "Peace," which many theater directors have interpreted as meaning "Silence!" but whose primary meaning is, Do not attack me, give me peace and serenity.

At their second meeting, when there might have been a way to help Lear understand and reason differently, Kent acts like an overprotective mother who caters to her child's every whim so as to keep him perennially dependent, even at the risk of his becoming dull and conceited. He does not alert him to his duties or help him to recognize his own overbearing aggressiveness—admittedly not an easy task.

Kent's later behavior particularly shows this hypothesis to be correct. He uses his brashness and caste arrogance (no character in the play is more aristocratic) not to defend the honor of his king (as he says and genuinely *believes*) but rather to alienate him altogether from his other daughters once Cordelia has removed herself as a rival. Kent, who has filial feelings for Lear ("Whom I have . . . loved as my father"), wants him to take back what he has given ("Revoke thy gift") (1.1.141, 163).

> See better, Lear, and let me still remain
> The true blank of thine eye. (1.1.158–59)

These words are wonderfully ambiguous, for they could be taken to mean, Look more carefully and let me go on being the only target at which you aim (in the world of archery "blank" can also mean "bull's eye"), or else Kent is offering himself as *sole* friend and adviser to the sovereign: Let me go on being the very center of your eye (using "blank" in a figurative sense). I shall return to this point below. Has Cordelia compelled Lear's attention? Kent outmaneuvers her with dexterity and manages to put her in the shadow with a few well-timed remarks.

He repeatedly offers his bluntness and sincerity as credentials, selling himself as an uncomplicated being:

> *Lear* What services canst do?
> *Kent* I can keep honest counsel, ride, run, mar a curious
> tale in telling it, and deliver a plain message bluntly. (1.4.31–33)

Yet he always uses remarkably ambiguous words and expressions—"mar," "curious," "bluntly": "mar a curious tale" could mean that he is artless; yet at the same time a curious tale stimulates curiosity, so it is as if he were admitting that he can transform a tale that is full of information and make a complete mess of it; to deliver a plain message bluntly might also mean to deliver a sharp blow to a simple message and thus destroy it. Kent gives the impression of being at once astute and naïve. Shakespeare seems to share this impression, having Cornwall speak the following words:

> This is some fellow
> Who, having been praised for bluntness, doth affect
> A saucy roughness, and constrains the garb
> Quite from his nature. He cannot flatter, he,
> An honest mind and plain, he must speak truth:
> And they will take't, so; if not, he's plain. (2.2.93–98)

There is one scene, however, that portrays him better than any other. Having been nominated the king's messenger to Regan and Cornwall, Kent violates the sacredness of his embassy in a manner that is as skillful as it is serious. Like the true aristocrat he is, he mistreats the yeoman Oswald and puts himself exaggeratedly (but not gratuitously) in conflict with Lear's last possible children. What matters above all is that (consciously or otherwise) his behavior constitutes a betrayal of the king's trust. And Lear recognizes it as such.

First, let us consider a few details from the preceding scenes. After the quarrel with Goneril, Lear is obviously worried. He clearly has feelings of guilt—so much so that he admits (apparently with reference to Regan), "I did her wrong" (1.5.25). The affirmation is important to the economy of the king's personal tragedy, since it is an admission that *he* might have done wrong to one of the two monsters of ingratitude. It is no mere chance that the Fool hastens to confuse him with puns and insults (1.5.2–51).

Lear is anxious, then, and wishes to win back at least Regan. To this end he hurriedly sends Kent with the explicit task of bringing his daughter and Cornwall *over to his side*. But although he has shown himself capable of swallowing his indignation whenever he thinks it best for himself, how does Kent react? First of all he engages in a quarrel with Goneril's messenger and then rounds things off by clashing with Regan and Cornwall:

Cornwall	Why dost thou call him knave?
	What is his fault?
Kent	His countenance likes me not.
Cornwall	No more perchance does mine, nor his, nor hers.
Kent	Sir, 'tis my occupation to be plain:
	I have seen better faces in my time
	Than stands on any shoulder that I see
	Before me at this instant. (2.2.87–94)

It must be admitted that Kent had warned his king: "I can keep an honest counsel . . . and deliver a plain message bluntly."

At any rate Regan and Cornwall fall into the trap and consign him to the stocks. Only then, and not before, does Kent rage about the insult "to his lord" and remind them of an ambassador's inviolability. But when Gloucester sees him in the stocks and offers to intercede on his behalf, Kent hurriedly dissuades him:

> Pray do not sir.
>
> . . . .
>
> A good man's fortune may grow out at heels. (2.2.146–48)

It is tempting to suggest that Kent is a mixture of ingenuousness and Machiavellianism—what might be called a split Machiavellianism (that is to say, totally remote from his consciousness), which has caused a critic as intelligent and able as Paul A. Jorgensen to assert that Kent is the least complex of *King Lear*'s characters.[66] Clinically speaking, however, he probably belongs to the category of perverse individuals with a dual personality, a complex personality that is by no means exhaustively defined (in Kent's own words) as "having more man than wit" (2.2.218). He is more precisely an "as if" personality: Kent behaves *as if* he were a noble and loyal human being, and yet he is not, or at least he would sincerely like to behave nobly but is unable to live up to his ideal.[67] However, he is not aware of his own deviousness. He is a politician, and a dangerous one, too. At the end of the play he confides to Cordelia:

> Yet to be known shortens my made intent. (4.6.9)

Critics have often wondered what plan he had in mind, given that he keeps it secret even when there is no apparent reason to do so. Kent's secret design—secret for him, too, being perhaps an unconscious design—is most probably to replace the three daughters in the king's affections, with the whole plan culminating in a great scene of reconciliation. In order to do this, he must separate the daughters from their father. Kent's hatred for Oswald is excessive—a paranoid hatred—while the steward himself is totally loyal to Goneril. Presumably Kent is so hostile toward him because he has projected onto him the part of himself that wants to sever the ties between father and daughters:

> Such smiling rogues as these,
> Like rats, oft bite the holy cords a-twain,
> Which are too intrince t'unloose. . . . (2.2.73–75)[68]

Kent also gnaws at the holy cords, just like the rats (which do not do their work in daylight). According to Kent's accusations, Oswald *smoothes*[69] his master's rage, pours oil on the fire, and then comes to cool it down when it has already gone out. This seems more like a portrait of Kent than of modest Oswald.

The habit of projecting feelings onto others is typical of paranoid subjects, as is the tendency to see "cold looks" (2.2.213) where they do not really exist (a point that will need further consideration). At the end of the "holy cords" speech, Kent (who has already outclassed Cordelia) proceeds to alienate Regan. When the king finds him in the stocks he asks: "What's he that hath so much thy place mistook / To set thee here?" (2.2.194–95). Kent does not give a true account of what has happened. Instead his brusque reply turns the situation to his advantage: "It is both he and she: / Your son and daughter" (2.2.196–97).

It is interesting to note that Lear does not believe him. Might this be because he knows Regan and Cornwall and is beginning to sense Kent's true nature? In order to try to demonstrate this point it would therefore be useful to consider the whole exchange from beginning to end:

Lear What's he that hath so much thy place mistook
    To set thee here?
Kent   It is both he and she:
    Your son and daughter.
Lear   No.
Kent   Yes.
Lear   No, I say.
Kent I say yea.
Lear   By Jupiter, I swear no!
Kent By Juno, I swear ay!
Lear   They durst not do't,
    They could not, would not do't; 'tis worse than murder,
    To do upon respect such violent outrage.

Resolve me with all modest haste which way
Thou mightst deserve or they impose this usage,
Coming from us. (2.2.194–203)

Although Kent swears by Juno, he does not give the true version of what happened: he omits to place events in their proper context and, above all, does not offer any explanation for having insulted Regan and Cornwall. The earlier scene with Regan, Cornwall, and Oswald would have needed to be entirely different to justify Kent's behavior.

Let us consider the episode. Oswald is most certainly lying when he claims to have been beaten by Lear because of "misconstruction." When he tells Cornwall that he has spared Kent "at suit of his grey beard" (2.2.62), he shows himself to be nothing more than an arrogant braggart, for he had actually been afraid that Kent might kill him. Nevertheless, when he encounters Kent a second time at Regan's court, he greets him with great courtesy. (He will admit to having been tripped up by Kent only after Kent has reminded him of it):

Oswald   Good dawning to thee, friend. Art of this house?
Kent   Ay.
Oswald   Where may we set our horses?
Kent   I' th' mire.
Oswald   Prithee, if thou lov'st me, tell me.
Kent   I love thee not.
Oswald   Why then, I care not for thee. (2.2.1–7)

Not only is Oswald polite to Kent but he clearly does not recognize him and even seems to take him for a member of Cornwall's court. The account Kent gives to Lear clearly contrasts sharply both with Oswald's courtesy and with other details:

My lord, when at their home
I did commend your highness' letters to them,
Ere I was risen from the place that showed
My duty kneeling, came there a reeking post
Stewed in his haste, half breathless, panting forth
From Goneril, his mistress, salutations,

Delivered letters spite of intermission,
Which presently they read, on whose contents
They summoned up their meiny, straight took horse,
Commanded me to follow and attend
The leisure of their answer, gave me cold looks;
And meeting here the other messenger,
Whose welcome I perceived had poisoned mine—
Being the very fellow which of late
Displayed so saucily against your highness—
Having more man than wit about me, drew.
He raised the house with loud and coward cries.
Your son and daughter found this trespass worth
The shame which here it suffers. (2.2.203–21)

Is Kent telling the truth? We do not actually witness these events onstage. Kent certainly must have known about or seen the letter that Oswald had taken from Goneril to Regan, otherwise he could not have told the king about it. Besides, the sort of behavior that Kent vaguely describes reflects Goneril's order to be "slack of services" (1.3.9). But this does not mean that things actually happened exactly the way Kent describes them. We are given only Kent's word for it that the episode evolved in this way; but it is precisely with regard to Kent's word that doubts are beginning to accumulate.

If Regan and Cornwall really did give Kent "cold looks" because of Oswald's interference and also commanded him to follow without listening to what he had to say, why should Kent have answered at first *vaguely* and then with offensive provocation when Cornwall asked him why he detested Oswald?

Cornwall	Why dost thou call him knave?
	What is his fault?
Kent	His countenance likes me not.
Cornwall	No more perchance does mine, nor his, nor hers.
Kent	Sir, 'tis my occupation to be plain:
	I have seen better faces in my time
	Than stands on any shoulder that I see
	Before me at this instant. (2.2.87–94)

Surely this dialogue flatly contradicts the account given to Lear by Kent. Nor should it be forgotten that when Kent intervenes in defense of Cordelia's "plainness" in the opening scene, he shows that he is perfectly capable of expressing himself very precisely and effectively with a few blunt words. But when addressing Cornwall he also shows himself capable of using elegant sarcasm (2.2.57–59). Why, then, does he not explain his own reasons and those of the king he represents with the same clarity? The question is by no means unimportant.

Kent's account of how he and Oswald arrived with their letters has raised suspicion before now. Suffice it to remember that besides Lear's own incredulity (which might be dictated by blindness) the Gentleman immediately asks the following question when Kent has finished telling his story:

Gentleman   Made you no more offence but what you speak of?
Kent   None. (2.2.235–36)

In any case, Lear has already decided that he wants to meet Regan and Cornwall face to face: "Follow me not; stay here" (2.2.234). Does he change his mind because he senses that Kent is unreliable? The clearest indication that Kent has lied is to be found in remarks made by Oswald and Kent in act 2, scene 2, *after* Kent's relation of events to the king:

Oswald   Why, what a monstrous fellow art thou, thus to
           rail on one that is neither known of thee nor knows
           thee! (2.2.23–25)

If Kent's account (which is beginning to sound suspicious) were actually true, he might have answered: What are you talking about? We met just now when we delivered our letters to the Duke and Duchess of Cornwall. Instead he says:

What a brazen-faced varlet art thou, to deny thou
knowest me! Is it two days ago since I tripped up thy heels
and beat thee before the King? (2.2.26–28)

Is this simply one of the play's numerous inconsistencies? It seems unlikely. Shakespeare insists on the fact that although Kent recognizes Oswald, Oswald does not recognize him. It is made clear at the beginning of the scene and emphasized in the above speech.

I should like to conclude by returning to the hypothesis that Kent wants to be the apple of Lear's blind eyes, which brings us back to Kent's words: "let me still remain / The true blank of thine eye" (1.1.158–59). One further, rather fascinating etymological hypothesis might be suggested: the primary meaning of "blank" is "white"—hence an empty space, a space where something is lacking: for instance, the blind pupil in the eye. In this case, the latent meaning of the sentence could be, Let me continue to be the false counselor who wants you to be blind and separated from the daughters who are my rivals.

If this hypothesis is acceptable, it could further be suggested that Kent employs the masochistic technique of letting himself be put in the stocks in order to arouse anguish and indignation in Lear and thus strengthen the bond between them. When, with the support of the Fool, Kent manages to give all the details about his unsuccessful mission to Regan, the king groans:

O, how this mother swells up toward my heart! (2.2.231)[70]

Hecate, the evil mother, half witch and half goddess, who reigns over the darkness in Lear's heart, has been invoked by Kent's maneuvers and now threatens to suffocate the king.

Dissonance

The dissonance in the scene in which Kent decides to disclose his real identity to the king is painful: by now Kent and Lear are two totally different human beings. Few have perhaps grasped its pitiless, tragic beauty: an old man who has glimpsed things he had always refused to accept, and for this reason is slowly dying, denies recognition to the servant who has tricked him in vain.

Lear enters with Cordelia's lifeless body in his arms. He is distraught, but poor, small, pathetic Kent, who cannot see any needs but his own, wants a different ending, an ending meant for him alone: "Is this the promised end?" (5.3.238).

If this is the conclusion, he seems to say, then what was the point of all that disguise and effort, and of running the risk of being executed if discovered? His tired mind has room only for an image of Lear who, having recognized him, embraces him and raises him to the position of favorite child. So intense is his anticipation that Kent cannot even participate in the tragedy that surrounds him:

> This feather stirs. She lives. If it be so,
> It is a chance which does redeem all sorrows
> That ever I have felt. (5.3.240–42)

For the last time, Kent now comes between the father and one of his daughters. His exclamation, "O my good master!" echoes a very different earlier intervention. In the opening scene of the play, he had addressed the king as "Good my liege." Nemesis has arrived. Grief has turned the dragon's voracious wrath into lucid judgment: "Prithee, away," says Lear (5.3.243)—almost as if he were telling him to respect the "holy cords."

And what words come spontaneously to Lear when Edgar tells him the truth about "faithful" Kent? "A plague upon you, murderers, traitors all" (5.3.244). Traitors! Kent had certainly betrayed him in his most important mission. And what are Lear's next words?

> Who are you?
> Mine eyes are not o' th' best, I'll tell you straight. (5.3.253–54)

This also means that he does not look kindly on Kent. It does not occur to Kent that Lear, perhaps unconsciously, echoes the "eye" metaphor that Kent himself had used; and so he steals in to depict himself as Lear's twin soul:

> If fortune brag of two she loved and hated,
> One of them we behold. (5.3.255–56)[71]

He does not understand. But Lear, declaring himself half blind, finally recognizes him:

> This' a dull sight.
> Are you not Kent? (5.3.256–57)

To give a somewhat brutal interpretation, "This' a dull sight" may also mean, This is a dreary vision. Kent obviously does not want to hear, for Lear has called him by his true name! This is "the promised end"! Kent replies:

> The same, your servant Kent.
> Where is your servant Caius? (5.3.258–59)

In the way that Alcibiades takes a deranged head for an empty one, Kent treats Lear as if he were a demented child: I am Kent and that is Caius! Do you see? And Lear, who until now has held back the stroke, lets his pent-up rage fall as sharply as an axe:

> He's a good fellow, I can tell you that.
> He'll strike, and quickly too. He's dead and rotten. (5.3.260–61)

"He's a good fellow," Shakespeare has him say, I assure you, he's good at fighting, and quick, too. "He's dead and *rotten.*" Lear reminds Kent that he has been the instrument of his violence; but Lear now repudiates violence. The word "dead" seems to imply that they no longer have anything in common; with the ambiguous "rotten," he is also accusing Kent of being corrupt and pitiful.[72]

But Kent still does not understand. He sees Lear as just a slow-witted old man who fails to see the sun shining before him, so he goes on insisting: "No, my good Lord; I am the very man" (5.3.262). The king's reply is both cold and enigmatic: "I'll see that straight" (5.3.263)—meaning "I'll see to that," but sounding like "Go away: the time for this sort of thing is past." Kent will obtain power, but will fail to achieve his only real purpose: the conquest of Lear's heart.[73]

The Two Monsters of Ingratitude

Even in the case of Goneril and Regan, the two "monsters of ingratitude," who have been the object of endless vituperation, a few natural stereotypes might be found at work. First, however, something needs to be said about the remarkable historical implications of *King Lear*.[74] Shakespeare quite consciously "historicizes" his plays. Suffice it to recall Hamlet's words to the players: the task of dramatic art is to show "the very age and body of the time, his form and pressure."[75] As for the actual period in which *King Lear* is set, Shakespeare playfully has the Fool say, "this prophecy Merlin shall make, for I live before his time" (3.2.95).

The political and cultural revolution of the sixteenth century and the phenomenon of colonial expansion gradually came to have their effect on the family. From the second half of the fifteenth century, Europe (England included) saw a strengthening of the state and a decline of the fragmented, arbitrary type of power that had been characteristic of medieval decentralization. The monarch was increasingly required to fulfill the function of the nation's interpreter and symbol in relation to foreign countries and to guarantee internal peace, law, and order. The merchant middle class also acquired economic and political power. All such changes encouraged the development of a secular mentality and a critical spirit, while the rise of the figure of the entrepreneur created a mentality capable of both initiative and planning.

King Lear strongly reflects many of the conflicts peculiar to the sixteenth and seventeenth centuries and dramatizes the new position of the family in the framework of sentimental life. This was an age of important changes in family attitudes toward children. In *The Babees Book* (1868), Frederich J. Furnivall quotes an Italian fifteenth-century text as stating that the heartlessness of the English is particularly evident in their attitude toward children.[76] Having kept them at home until the age of seven, eight, or even nine, rather than sending them to school or introducing them into the adult world, they send them to live in other households, where they remain until the age of fourteen, and sometimes as late as eighteen. The Italian writer's insinuation is that the English resorted to keeping other people's children in order to obtain better service. However, they rationalized all this in the name of "learning good manners." Philippe Ariès observes that although the Italian writer implies that such customs are unknown in his own country this kind of arrangement was probably quite common in the medieval Western world.[77]

In a more general sense, the main duty of a child who had been entrusted to a tutor was to serve him well. In the fifteenth century, with the advent of schooling as we know it, family realities and feelings began to change. This slow but profound revolution, which contemporaries (historians, for example) largely overlooked, seems to have been difficult to acknowledge.

The changing structure of family morality nevertheless began to assume a well-defined shape, also regarding the ancient custom of having a favorite child, as Lear did. According to Ariès, the concept of the privileged child, whether due to primogeniture or simple parental favor, was a fundamental part of family life from the late Middle Ages through to the seventeenth century. In the second half of the seventeenth century, educational theorists began to question the legitimacy of this practice both because it conflicted with the new demand for equal rights to family affection and because it involved the secular use of ecclesiastical benefits. In *De l'éducation chrétienne des enfants*, published in 1666 (sixty years after *King Lear*), A. Varet devoted a whole chapter (possibly the first ever on the subject) to "l'égalité qu'il faut garder entre les enfants" (the need to treat children without discrimination or favoritism).[78]

Another of the major themes of *King Lear* concerns the disastrous consequences that are likely to follow the division of a kingdom. This was connected with the politicodidactic preoccupations of the time, which stemmed from the need to consolidate national unity, after centuries of feudal divisions and civil wars. *Gorbobuc,* one of the first and most important Elizabethan tragedies, is a dramatization of this very theme.[79] The success of Tudor politics had been to bring the whole country under the control of a central administration as well as to defeat the aristocratic rebellion—a process that did not begin until the late sixteenth century.

To return to Goneril and Regan: If this historical and political background is taken properly into account, certain events may take on quite a different significance. Lear's elder daughters will turn out to be monsters, but are they monsters of ingratitude? Does their cruelty derive from their treacherous and evil nature, as Cordelia insists? Or have they been contaminated by Lear's own cruelty?

Although it is true that Gloucester is cruelly blinded, it is also true that he had previously been trusted and held in esteem by both Cornwall and Regan. Indeed, Regan had apprehensively turned to him, with Goneril's encouragement, for help in resolving the conflict between her duty to maintain both her self-respect as queen and her childhood ties with her father, which would mean having to submit to his bullying:

> Occasions, noble Gloucester, of some poise,
> Wherein we must have use of your advice,
> Our father he hath writ, so hath our sister,
> Of differences which I least thought it fit
> To answer from our home. The several messengers
> From hence attend dispatch. Our good old friend,
> Lay comforts to your bosom, and bestow
> Your needful counsel to our businesses,
> Which craves the instant use. (2.1.119–27)

Gloucester betrays her esteem and trust, and at the same time betrays his country. Nor does he do this with noble intent but, rather, (the context suggests) out of pure opportunism:

> . . . I have received a letter this night—'tis dangerous to be
> spoken—I have locked the letter in my closet. These
> injuries the King now bears will be revenged home.
> There is part of a power already footed. We must incline
> to the King. (3.3.10–14)

Where the behavior of the two queens is concerned, the moralistic approach is one of the obstinate stereotyped responses, but it does not really hold good since it distorts the tragic nature of events. Still, it is worth trying to follow its reasoning. Before ingratitude can exist, an authentic gift must have been made. In the allegorical scheme common to all fairy tales, the kingdom and the crown can be taken as symbols of the right to human dignity and individual self-fulfillment. In the logic of maturity, gifts are either given or not given—after all, Lear was under no obligation to abdicate.

According to this logic, contracts made by the "major" party must consider the interests of the "minor," otherwise there is no contract but an abuse of power disguised as liberality. And bullying not only can but must be prevented, irrespective of its perpetrator.

Among the conditions for the transfer of his kingdom, the sovereign had unilaterally demanded the right to keep a hundred knights and his royal title. Did he unconsciously fear that without such instruments of power (only the latter of which is symbolic), he risked being persecuted and despoiled by his daughters? And yet the maintenance of the prerogatives of royal power appears to be not only unjust but also illogical, for, as Louis XIV stated, there is "nothing more contemptible than to see all the power on one side and the mere title of king on the other."[80] If the play is considered in the light of this observation, it seems quite clear that Lear expects to go on behaving like a spoiled child with impunity, a child who mocks both the authority and the dignity of his daughters in their own house. And he does all this through "generosity." Moreover, he leaves his daughters with the burden of administering the kingdom, of maintaining internal order and defending the country from foreign foes. How can the two queens possibly be respected by their subjects when their father constantly humiliates them in public?

Lear's behavior implies double-bind communication,[81] structurally contradictory speech that can lead directly to madness. Why, then, does Lear behave in this way? His insecurity leads him continually to torment those whom he would like to trust but whom he fears to lose because of his affective insatiability. It might be suggested that giving away his kingdom conceals Lear's wish to tighten the hold on his daughters so that he will have them constantly at his disposal. He expects to receive unlimited sacrifices.

At the beginning, it is he who behaves like the legendary pelican mother who makes endless sacrifices for her young: although she even offers them the flesh of her own breast, this is basically an expedient to keep them dependent and eventually blackmail them by making them feel guilty through her accusations of neglect and ingratitude.[82] Is this the "darker purpose" (1.1.36) that Lear mentions when he is sharing out the kingdom?

Text or Performance?

Despite everything that has reasonably been said about them, both Goneril and Regan (the latter is a more ambiguous figure and really deserves further analysis) do show fundamental attitudes that can be defined as mature.[83] Unlike their younger sister, who seems always to have feared and hated them, Goneril and Regan see their father's behavior toward Cordelia and Kent as alarming because it is dictated by "poor judgement" and "unconstant starts" (1.1.290, 299). Nonetheless (perhaps out of self-interest), they do not intervene on behalf of either their sister or Kent. They refuse to accept the blackmail implicit in Lear's pelican-mother devotion, which is a healthy sign. They must defend their own integrity and are far from having the altruism needed to soothe their father's madness.[84]

Their theatrical destiny has been marked by the disagreeable impression made on the audience by their flattery: the predictable dramatic mechanism comes inexorably into play, leaving us no time to reflect upon Lear's long-standing authoritarian nature. Given such a nature, it can reasonably be assumed that his daughters have been raised in a despotic yet probably seductive atmosphere; they have grown up with the conviction that they must be submissive at all times or be repudiated. This is no mean threat.[85]

However, theatrical suggestion also obscures the fact that on a level that is in a sense magical and ephemeral, their grandiloquent words of praise fulfill Lear's real, primitive needs. And the fact that this has not been emphasized again reveals the way in which the reader or spectator can be led astray.

The Italian actor and director Giorgio Albertazzi based his 1992 production of *Lear* at the Teatro Greco at Taormina on my interpretation, proving (if nothing else) that the director's interpretative key decides from the very start whether Goneril and Regan are false and hypocritical. Goneril is a determined woman:

> . . . Old fools are babes again, and must be used
> With checks as flatteries, when they are abus'd. (1.3.20–21)

Those "flatteries" are an explicit reference to what she and Regan say to their father in the first scene. Goneril's mistake is to believe in the pedagogical strategy of the stick and the carrot, and (it must be stressed) to overlook the fact that the child in Lear has far more serious anxieties than she imagines. She does, however, make some attempt to respond.

In the opening scene, Lear demands like a child, and Goneril and Regan respond like mothers. Cordelia, on the contrary, responds like a child: her demands are in conflict with Lear's. He speaks to her as if she were a mother. Instead of the "nursery" he expects from her, he finds the "empty space" waiting to engulf him.[86] Lear is terrified of his empty, worthless self, but what does Cordelia offer him? "Nothing." Hers is a mortal threat, an incredibly violent attack. Thus, it has been seen that when Kent sides with Cordelia, the word "Peace!" comes naturally to the king's lips.

The two "horrible ingrates" realize that their father's violence is an authentic danger, but they do not turn him into a dragon (or only to a limited extent). On the contrary, they (particularly Goneril) continually attempt to make him reason on the basis of an inadequate but firm and realistic logic:

> *Goneril* Not only, sir, this your all-licensed fool,
> But other of your insolent retinue
> Do hourly carp and quarrel, breaking forth
> In rank and not-to-be-endurèd riots. Sir,
> I had thought by making this well known unto you,
> To have found a safe redress, but now grow fearful,
> By what yourself too late have spoke and done,

That you protect this course, and put in on
By your allowance; which if you should, the fault
Would not scape censure, nor the redresses sleep,
Which in the tender of a wholesome weal
Might in their working do you that offence,
Which else were shame, that then necessity
Will call discreet proceeding.

. . . .

Lear   Are you our daughter?

Goneril I would you would make use of your good wisdom,
Whereof I know you are fraught, and put away
These dispositions which of late transport you
From what you rightly are.

. . . .

Lear   Your name, fair gentlewoman?

Goneril This admiration, sir, is much o' th' savour
Of other your new pranks. I do beseech you
To understand my purposes aright,
As you are old and reverend, should be wise. (1.4.183–96, 201–
5, 214–18)

Having received their investiture (emancipation, the prerequisite of an adult's self-respect), Goneril and Regan cannot and must not renounce it, for to do so would amount to suicidal regression: those who renounce maturity are punished with folly. When Albany says, "See thyself devil!" Goneril replies to him dryly, "O vain fool!" (4.4.35, 37).

Theirs, of course, is a very sketchy and obviously a very fragile kind of maturity. They might, however, resort to deception, not so much because they are innately perverse but because they know no better means; indeed, perhaps there were no better means in that particular situation. What must be kept clearly in mind is the culture of that period (along with its dangerous subspecies, public opinion) and, more important still, the kind of childhood Goneril and Regan probably had, together with the overwhelming response of their father. All such factors work against their potential emancipation.

As we have seen, Lear constantly plays one daughter off against the other. He insists on seeing them during the moments of greatest tension early in the play. It is typical of the despot to seek head-on confrontations in the hope of evoking the flames and poisonous vapors of the dragon to terrify and subdue the "rebel." Cornwall and Regan sensibly attempt to avoid confrontation, but they do not necessarily do so out of cowardice. According to Lear, their refusal to show themselves is a challenge to his power: it is an attack against the master, against the arrogant infant-king. Another fairly realistic hypothesis might be that Albany and Regan know how furious they are at the king's overbearing attitude. Since they also know that they are stronger, their refusal to clash with him is a way of protecting him from the worst.

However, this is not exactly how things stand, for the two sisters, too, have a hidden need that binds them to old Lear, even though they are not conscious of it. Goneril's error, if it can be called that, is to alternate between a "parental" attitude comprising a mixture of perverse blandishments and severity and an adult attitude that requires mutual respect. This she does while failing to understand that before her stands a man who is on the verge of madness.[87] At another level, the two sisters feel so harassed by their father that they respond with extreme ferocity—the very ferocity of Lear himself.[88]

In many ways, Bradley is the founder of the type of critical approach I am proposing here—not cold reason but comparison, analysis, and dissection. And yet with regard to this particular aspect of the tragedy, my disagreement with him could not be more radical. What is Iago's wickedness against the envied foreigner, Bradley wonders, compared with the cruelty of Gloucester's son and Lear's daughters? What is the suffering of a strong man like Othello compared with that of a vulnerable old man?[89]

There is evidence here of an ideological outlook reflecting the moralistic dynamics of the ascribing of guilt in Manichean terms. Bradley does not grasp the fact that the family metaphor of *King Lear* expresses one of the most controversial issues of Shakespeare's time: the problem of freedom of thought and action,

John Fisher and Thomas More in opposition to Henry VIII, and Henry VIII himself to the Church of Rome.

Some critics still believe that *Lear* is set in a timeless period, which is certainly true as far as the laws governing "damn'd melancholy" are concerned.[90] In this play, Shakespeare dramatizes the more or less hidden, far-reaching process involving the secularization of English politics, which was brought to the surface by the Pareus case, barely fifteen years after the first performance of *Lear*, following the dissolution of the most important of James I's parliaments on 6 January 1622.[91] Pareus may be seen as symbol of the confrontation between court and country. In a sermon preached at Saint Paul's Cross in July 1622, Montaigne, the Bishop of London, condemned Pareus's heresy against the state, for Pareus had dared to place "the authority of the people" above that of "tyrannical princes." David Owen also denounced Pareus's opinion that fundamental laws were "contracts" between princes and people and that violation of these absolved the people from religious or legal obligation to the ruler, who could then rightly be stripped of authority. Owen found this scandalous and insisted on the habitual doctrine of obedience, according to which all tyranny, whether it offends God or Man, must be tolerated and can be suppressed by God alone. Tyranny, claimed Owen, was both God's punishment for impiety and a test of faith: cruel tyrants were therefore a just scourge, while clement princes were a divine reward for piety. This is a familiar Elizabethan doctrine, as in the homily on obedience regularly read in church.

Lear had said, "we will divest us both of rule, / Interest of territory, cares of state" (1.1.49–50),[92] and Goneril, as head of this state, cannot accept that her father "would manage those authorities / That he hath given away" (Q. 3.17–18).[93]

The Bastard

Blindness is everywhere. Let us consider Edmond, as well as Lear's "old age." A close look at the lines in which Gloucester introduces Edmond to Kent will show that certain impressions cannot be refuted:

Kent	Is not this your son, my lord?
Gloucester	His breeding, sir, hath been at my charge. I have so often blushed to acknowledge him, that now I am brazed to do it.
Kent	I cannot conceive you.
Gloucester	Sir, this young fellow's mother could, whereupon she grew round-wombed, and had, indeed, sir, a son for her cradle ere she had a husband for her bed. Do you smell a fault?
Kent	I cannot wish the fault undone, the issue of it being so proper.
Gloucester	But I have a son, sir, by order of law, some year older than this, who yet is no dearer in my account. Though this knave came something saucily to the world before he was sent for, yet was his mother fair, there was good sport at his making, and the whoreson must be acknowledged. Do you know this noble gentleman, Edmond? (1.1.7–24)

Edmond has been surrounded by violence and contradiction ever since he was born. In the totally insensitive language typical of many men of that time (including Lear), he was told that he had come into the world by mistake, that making love to his mother had been "good sport," and that she was at best a worthless, irresponsible woman and at worst a real whore.[94] Gloucester quite clearly says that Edmond would have been a social outcast if he had not happened to have a generous and broad-minded father! It is no wonder, then, that Edmond's vengeance is dedicated to a mother:

Thou, nature, art my goddess. To thy law
My services are bound. (1.2.1–2)[95]

As for Lear's vulnerable old age, Bradley is not aware that there is also a type of senility that is aggravated by hysteria or that a man who goes hunting with his faithful attendants (1.3.8) and in the end kills his daughter's assassin with a sword (5.3.249) may rightly be suspected of not being totally decrepit. At most, Lear is mentally old.

It is indeed because Lear has not fulfilled himself as a human being capable of adult affection, with a sense of justice or the kind of sensitivity that I have emphasized, that he is unable to appreciate his daughters' needs or qualities. Like many people who have suffered arrested development, Lear denies his need for love, denies being unable to find it, and therefore resorts to staging the initial pantomime and proclaiming his rights.[96] At the same time, it has been seen that Goneril and Regan confusedly search for a "constitutional" father—just as there would subsequently be constitutional kings and just as Henry VIII had also wanted a "constitutional" pope. As Edgar claims, "Ripeness is all" (5.2.11).

From time immemorial, the administration of law and justice according to merit has been the characteristic duty or, rather, contribution of a father. Yet Lear, as a father, betrays this expectation. He might be called an unnatural father, for he turns out to be a possessive, irrational, and unpredictable child-father, one who gives today and takes away tomorrow.

Goneril's rebellion is an attempt to recover some of the power that she has already transferred by natural proxy to her father, who has betrayed his mandate. Why, then, does she fail? Perhaps one reason can be identified. Lear ought to have set her free gradually and without second thoughts; instead he does so suddenly and in a purely formal manner.

Those who have social and institutional power, symbolized by the various Gloucesters and Kents of this world, who have the impressive force of ideology at their disposal (both could be considered counselors to the king), stand in the way of the desire of the individual to recover his or her alienated power. These figures have an important influence on events in the tragedy. Are the daughters afraid of freedom? Regan's hesitations and Goneril's drastic conclusions are signs of their insecurity. They still harbor a strong desire to revive, at a social level, a flesh-and-blood father able to protect them from the primitive terror evoked by the dragon, as well as another Saint George father figure able to alleviate their feelings of guilt toward a parent who has been attacked and is furious.

Does their sudden, theatrically abrupt and almost gratuitous love for Edmond the bastard express this compelling need? So ambiguous and three-sided, so riddled with jealousy is the two sisters' *coup de foudre* that it does not even seem ambiguous: it is clearly and desperately Oedipal. Being creatures of flesh and blood like the rest of us, Goneril and Regan not only despise and hate their father but also love him in the vehement, conflict-ridden, and unresolved way they have learned from Lear himself. He is the true "bastard," in need of the immense amount of attention that alone will heal the wounds of childhood. What they love about Edmond is the fact that he is a bastard, un-acknowledged, a derelict. What words does he utter when he is dying? "Yet Edmond was beloved" (5.3.215). These words echo the show of affection exacted by Lear.

This *coup de foudre* allows Goneril and Regan to continue their attempt to keep love separate from rage. While Lear continues to be the object of their hatred for a tyrannical father, the primal love for a father who (Lear gives us to understand) had once known how to be warm and passionate is transferred to Edmond. This process of splitting avoids the depression that would have set in (and was quite probably about to set in, so providential is their sudden love for Gloucester's bastard son) as soon as the two figures of the father began to merge into one. In order to avoid a torment so devastating that it cannot always be overcome by splitting, Shakespeare applied the only balm he could imagine:

"Though death be poor it ends a mortal woe."[97]

Notes

Foreword

1. Umberto Eco, *The Limits of Interpretation* (Bloomington: Indiana University Press, 1990).

Preface

1. Gustave Flaubert, *Correspondance,* 9 vols. (Paris: L. Conard, 1926–33), 3:45. Quotations taken from the Pléiade edition of Flaubert's *Correspondance,* 3 vols. (Paris: Gallimard, 1973–91), will be referred to as *Correspondance,* Pléiade. Unless otherwise indicated, all translations from the French are the editor's or the translator's.

Charbovari: An Essay on *Madame Bovary*

1. Gustave Flaubert, *Madame Bovary,* edited with variants and notes by Claudine Gothot-Mersch (Paris: Classiques Garnier, Bordas, 1990), 372. In its context the now obsolete expression means, "Charles and Emma were socially self-sufficient." Hereafter, page references will appear parenthetically in the text. Unless otherwise indicated, quotes from *Madame Bovary* are from "Livre de Poche" (Paris: Librairie Générale Française, 1983).

2. It is also true to say that stereotypes form part of the mechanisms of the formation and transmission of cultures and of the ideologies inherent in scientific discourse.

3. See Paul Antony Tanner, *Adultery in the Novel* (Baltimore: Johns Hopkins Press, 1979), 254 on the three Mesdames Bovary.

4. Quotations from *Madame Bovary* in English are taken from Geoffrey Wall's translation (Harmondsworth: Penguin, 1992). A few very minor modifications have been made.

5. The term "bovarysme" was almost certainly coined by Jules Barbey d'Aurevilly, who employed it in a review in 1862. Jules de Gaultier's *Bovarysme: La Psychologie dans l'oeuvre de Flaubert* first appeared in 1892 and was republished in *Bovarysme* in 1902 (Paris: Mercure de France). See Stephen Heath, *Gustave Flaubert's Madame Bovary* (Cambridge: Cambridge University Press, 1992).

6. De Gaultier, *Bovarysme,* 1–2.

7. Flaubert, quoted in Heath, *Gustave,* 95. Heath comments: "In the

writing of Emma, Flaubert achieved something as radical as it was scandalous: a new conception of the feminine, of woman. . . . Once again, it was Baudelaire who immediately recognized this when he praised Flaubert's novel for providing the great literary document of hysteria: "Hysteria! Why should not this physiological mystery be the matter and bedrock of a literary work, this mystery that the Academy of Medicine has not yet resolved?" Flaubert replied that Baudelaire had penetrated the arcane in the book (21 October 1857). Incidentally, when Baudelaire himself was accused of having published obscenities, the public prosecutor happened to be Ernest Pinard, who had also spoken for the state against *Madame Bovary*.

8. Sénard quoted in "Les Procès de *Madame Bovary*," in Gustave Flaubert, *Oeuvres complètes*, edited by Bernard Masson, 2 vols. (Paris: Editions du Seuil, 1964), 2:724–50.

9. Albert Thibaudet, *Gustave Flaubert* (Paris: Gallimard, 1935).

10. Ibid., 105.

11. Vladimir Nabokov, *Lectures on Literature* (New York: Harvest/HBJ Books, 1980). Félicien Marceau, preface to *Madame Bovary* (Paris: Librairie Générale Française, 1961), 5–11.

12. Algirdas Julien Greimas, *Du sens II: Essais sémiotiques* (Paris: Editions du Seuil, 1983). Gérard Genette, *Figures III* (Paris: Editions du Seuil, 1972). Victor Brombert comments: "One almost has the impression that Flaubert enjoyed destroying Charles professionally. (Is there a hint here of a secret animosity toward his father?)" *The Novels of Flaubert* (Princeton: Princeton University Press, 1966), 73.

13. Jean-Paul Sartre, *Les Mots* (Paris: Gallimard, 1964), 49–50.

14. The first volume of *L'Idiot de la famille* was published by Gallimard in 1971. Sartre had intended it to be a study of Flaubert's life from 1821 to 1857, but it was never completed. In his preface to the first volume Sartre wrote: "Anybody will tell you that *Madame Bovary* was written by Gustave Flaubert. But what is the relationship between the man and his work? I have not yet explained it and neither has anyone else as far as I know. It will turn out to be double-sided: *Madame Bovary* is both a defeat and a victory" (8).

15. Maurice Bardèche, "Des documents aux scénarios," introduction to Gustave Flaubert, *Madame Bovary* (Paris: Librairie Générale Française, 1972), 516.

16. The scenario is, however, more complex. One recurrent characteristic of hysterical women who find themselves in a psychological state similar to Emma's is that they suffer great fear of being abandoned from their earliest infancy. They are unable to bear the severing of a bond, even though they actually detest it. As soon as they unconsciously conceive the idea (however vaguely) of leaving their husbands, their ten-

dency is to give birth to a child, onto whom they can (again unconsciously) project all their anxious need for dependence.

17. In coldly clinical terms, it could be said that Emma's neurosis is also a conflictual attempt to communicate her own suffering. Charles's "illness," on the other hand, is a personality disorder. He is a moral masochist and his behavior is a mixture of what are known as "reaction formations."

18. Flaubert, *Correspondance* Pléiade, 2:483–86.

19. Gustave Flaubert, *Madame Bovary* (Paris: Michel Lévy Frères, 1857), 9:221.

20. See, e.g., the Larousse *Dictionnaire de la langue française.*

21. An edition with notes and variants, edited by Edouard Maynial, was also published in the Classiques Garnier in 1951. The 1990 Garnier edition, quoted in note 1, does not contain this variant.

22. Bardèche, Scénarios, xiv.

23. Sartre was of the opinion that for Flaubert *Madame Bovary* was "both a defeat and a victory" (*L'Idiot,* 1:8). See also "Le 'qui perd gagne' rationalisé," in ibid., 2:1923ff. The psychoanalyst Theodor Reik synthesized the essential features of the compulsive behavior of moral masochists with the formula "victory through defeat." His *Masochism in Modern Man* (New York: Farrar Straus, 1941) is perhaps the first work to deal with the phenomenological portrayal of moral masochists. Reik's observations remain valid to this day: moral masochists always manage to ruin both work and play in whatever activity they undertake; they deny themselves the happiness they deserve and in extreme cases they even put their own lives in jeopardy. In most cases, it may seem to the casual observer that the bad luck and misfortunes in the lives of such people are due to external causes, as if they had constantly had to fight the events and accursed disasters that keep dogging their destinies. How many admirers of this novel have believed that Emma's yearnings were the cause of Charles's misfortunes?

24. Gustave Flaubert, *Mémoires d'un Fou,* in *Oeuvres,* 1:233.

25. The psychoanalytic term for this phenomenon is projective identification. I shall pay greater attention to it in the essay on *King Lear.*

26. Flaubert, *Correspondance,* 4:164. Flaubert is here speaking of the role of the writer, who "must be in his work like God in the Creation [doit être dans son oeuvre comme Dieu dans la Création]" (ibid.).

27. Sigmund Freud, *The Psychopathology of Everyday Life* (1901), in *The Standard Edition of the Complete Psychological Works of Sigmund Freud,* edited by James Strachey, 24 vols. (London: Hogarth Press, 1953–74), 6:162–89. Like *lapsus linguae,* parapraxes are disturbances caused by unconscious conflict in the performance of a commonplace mental function or voluntary physical act.

28. Flaubert, *Correspondance,* 3:45.

29. Theodor Reik, *Masochism,* realized that the moral masochist's sense of guilt sometimes reaches the conscious part of the mind—causing a disagreeable and irritating feeling that may, however, be quickly overcome.

30. This aspect of Emma—at times a self-imposed protective mother, at other times an immature and deliriously jealous child—would perhaps be sufficient reason to consider her a hysteric.

31. Flaubert, *Correspondance,* 1:240. I shall deal with ambivalence and other themes that are implied here in the essay on *King Lear.*

32. Technically speaking, it might be more accurate to say that a split part of him knows.

33. Theodor Reik (who may even have inspired Sartre in his preface to *L'Idiot de la famille*) listed the essential characteristics of such behavior under the already mentioned heading "Victory through Defeat" (see *Masochism,* chapter 30).

34. See Erich Auerbach, *Mimesis: Dargestellte Wirklichkeit in der Abenländischen Literatur* (Bern: Francke, 1946), 412, 428ff.

35. Flaubert, *Correspondance,* 3:77.

36. Reik devotes a whole chapter to the "suspense factor" (see *Masochism,* chapter 4).

37. Flaubert, *Correspondance,* 8:174.

38. I have already discussed the limitations of psychoanalysis as a critical tool in the preface to this volume.

39. Miguel de Unamuno, "Leyendo a Flaubert," in *Ensayos* (Madrid: Aguilar, 1964), 2:1038–39.

40. Flaubert, *Correspondance,* 4:164.

41. J. Heinrich Heine, *Mémoiren* (1884), quoted in Edmund Bergler, *Homosexuality: Disease or Way of Life?* (New York: Hill and Wang, 1956), 104.

42. Geneviève Mouillaud, "Le Bel Oedipe," in *Le Rouge et le noir de Stendhal* (Paris: Larousse, 1973), 175–84.

43. Bergler, *Homosexuality,* 104.

44. Enid Starkie, *The Making of the Master* (Harmondsworth: Penguin Books, 1971), 357.

45. I shall return to the problem of the relationship between author and characters and that of a character split into two or more figures (Charles was earlier identified with the tramp with Justin) in my essay on *King Lear.*

46. Eugène Delamare, a medical student of Flaubert's father, had gone out to a country practice. Here, after a first marriage to an older widow, he had married an ambitious farm girl, Delphine Couturier, whose affairs with other men soon became notorious. Delphine was young, a

nymphomaniac, and she committed suicide with arsenic. Louise Pradier ("Ludovica"), the wife of the sculptor James Pradier, separated from her husband as a result of a scandalous relationship she had had with a young man. Louise Colet was the first passion of Gustave's mature life, and became one of his main correspondents. For a discussion of Louise Colet as a model for Emma Bovary, see Benjamin F. Bart, *Flaubert* (Syracuse: Syracuse University Press, 1967), 156.

47. Jean Rousset, *Forme et signification* (Paris: J. Corti, 1963), 113.

48. Brombert, *Novels*, 41. He writes in his exceptional essay: "The collective personal *nous* ('We were in class when . . .') evidently communicates the proper tone of childhood reminiscences."

49. Sartre, *L'Idiot*, 1:83.

50. Gustave Flaubert, *Rage et impuissance* (1836), in *Oeuvres*, 1:83–87.

51. Caroline de Commanville, *Souvenirs intimes*, published as a preface to volume 1 of Flaubert, *Correspondance*, x–xi. Quoted also in the captivating biography of Gustave Flaubert written by Bart, *Flaubert*, 14.

52. Léon Daudet, *Le Stupide: XIXᵉ siècle* (Paris: Nouvelle Librairie Nationale, 1922).

53. P. M. Wetherill, *Flaubert et la création littéraire* (Paris: Librairie Nizet, 1964).

54. Flaubert, *Mémoires, Oeuvres*, 1:232.

55. Thibaudet, *Gustave*, 111.

56. Flaubert, *Correspondance*, 1:312.

57. Ibid., 3:372.

58. Gustave Flaubert, *Voyage en Orient*, in *Oeuvres*, 2:449–705.

59. Word of Arabic extraction meaning "bay window."

60. A slang expression alluding to the type of young male prostitute described here (defined by the *Trésor de la langue française* [1975] as a "jeune garçon dont les gens de moeurs lévantines abusent"). Flaubert uses the word frequently in his *Correspondance*, often as a term of endearment to his friends.

61. Flaubert underlines the words "It made me wet," an expression usually referring to female sexual excitement. "Vi" in the final paragraph stands for "vit," a vulgar term for penis (translated as "pri" for "prick").

    This letter appears as a footnote in the original edition of Starkie's *Making of the Master*. The same edition contains an introduction dating from 1966 in which the author comments on this and other letters (to Louis Bouilhet on 13 March 1850 and 12 August 1856, as well as to Louise Colet in December 1853) that it would be hard to believe that these passages, which have not appeared in previous editions, are not evidence of homosexual practice. At the same time, Starkie recalls that Gustave had told Madame Brainne that he was a son of Lesbos (*Correspondance*,

Supplément, 4 vols. [Paris: Conard, 1853], 4:287, letter dated 10–11 December 1879) and that he had addressed Bouilhet as "Vieux pédéraste" in a letter dated 2 October 1860 (*Correspondance,* 3:76). The passages in the letter quoted by Starkie vary in several places from the text I have quoted, from the Pléiade edition of the *Correspondance,* 1:567–76.

Confirmation that these aspects of Flaubert's personality were linked to serious anxieties and uncertain sexual identity is to be found in his *Souvenirs, notes et pensées intimes* (in Gustave Flaubert, *Oeuvres de jeunesse inédites,* 3 vols. [Paris: Conard, 1853], 3:182, 192, 195), where, at the age of nineteen, Flaubert mentions his desire to be a woman. In a letter to Louise Colet dated 22 December 1852 (*Correspondance,* 3:76)—to which I shall return later—he confirmed that when he was a student in Paris at the age of nineteen he had often wished to castrate himself.

62. Flaubert, *Correspondance,* 4:180.

63. Jean-Pierre Richard, *Littérature et sensation* (Paris: Editions du Seuil, 1954), 137.

64. Ibid., 137.

65. Flaubert, *Correspondance,* 3:269.

66. Gustave Flaubert, *La Tentation de Saint Antoine,* 1849 version (published for the first time in Paris, by Conard, in 1910), 226. All quotations from the 1849 version of *Tentation* are taken from Richard, *Littérature,* 137–56.

67. Flaubert, *Correspondance,* 2:47.

68. In chapter 1 of *Mimesis,* Erich Auerbach comments on one sentence from the novel: "But it was especially at meal times that she could bear it no longer, . . . all the bitterness of her life seemed to have been dished up on a plate."

69. René Dumesnil, *Gustave Flaubert, l'homme et l'oeuvre* (Paris: Desclée de Brouwer, 1932), 491.

70. Throughout the *Correspondance,* but especially in the letters to Louise Colet, Chatepie, and Alfred Le Poittevin, Flaubert speaks of his illness as if it were a "nervous disorder," an expression in vogue at that time; about his mother he said, "she has nervous fits accompanied by hallucinations, like the ones I had [elle a des attaques de nerfs, mêlées d'hallucinations comme j'en avais]" (*Correspondance,* 2:42). He attributes to himself, however, several symptoms that, as Hearth points out (see *Gustave,* 95), were diagnosed as symptoms of hysteria in the *Dictionnaire des sciences médicales* (which filled six shelves in Charles Bovary's study!). It is interesting to note that when speaking of his nervous fits, Flaubert remarks that "the psychic element then rises above me and consciousness disappears with the sense of being alive [L'élément psychique alors saute pardessus moi et la conscience disparait avec le sentiment de la vie]" (*Correspondance,* 3:77).

71. W. Ronald D. Fairbairn, *Psychoanalytical Studies on Personalities* (1952; reprint, London: Routledge, 1990), 86. From a modern psychoanalytic point of view, it would be better to speak of "pseudogenitality."

72. Flaubert, *Correspondance*, 2:209.

73. Flaubert, *Tentation* (1849), 273.

74. Flaubert, *Correspondance*, 1:201.

75. Flaubert, *Tentation* (1849), 324.

76. Flaubert, *Mémoires, Oeuvres*, 1:238.

77. Ibid., 1:233.

78. Ibid. The theme of "circles" is often found in Flaubert's work.

79. Ibid.

80. Flaubert, *Correspondance*, 1:208.

81. Victor Brombert, *Flaubert par lui-même* (Paris: Editions du Seuil, 1971), 9.

82. Words spoken by Hilarion in the definitive version of Gustave Flaubert, *Tentation de Saint Antoine*, in *Oeuvres*, 1:536.

83. "I want . . . to be in everything, emanate from odors, grow like plants, flow like water, vibrate like sound, shine like light, hide in all forms, penetrate every atom, descend into the depths of matter—to be matter! [Je voudrais . . . être en tout, m'émaner avec les odeurs, me développer comme les plantes, couler comme l'eau, vibrer comme le son, briller comme la lumière, me blottir sur toutes les formes, pénétrer chaque atome, descendre jusqu'au fond de la matière,—être la matière!]" Flaubert, *Tentation, Oeuvres*, 1:571.

84. Flaubert, *Correspondance*, 7:67.

85. Sigmund Freud, *The Economic Problem of Masochism, Standard Edition*, 1923 19:159–70.

86. See Brombert, *Flaubert*, 94.

87. Flaubert, *Correspondance*, 4:118.

88. I am here making only passing reference to a phenomenon that is rather more complex and might lead into a discussion of Flaubertian scatology. The exceedingly tormented search for words and phrases in Flaubert's style is (obviously only to a certain extent) attributable to the ritualized manner in which the obsessive personality tends to confront the possibility (fed by his own ambivalence) that something created by his own love might be destroyed by his own hatred. Words or sentences might betray an uncontrolled sadistic impulse and thus compromise the image of oneself that one wishes to project, but they can equally harm the reader through attacks that, in the imagination of obsessive writers, are not infrequently represented by fecal explosions.

In this respect, Flaubert's constant dissatisfaction may well testify to the failure of the process of ritualization so typical of such neuroses. The compulsive need to repeat formalities is linked with the continued failure of defense mechanisms. The drafting and editing of *Madame Bovary*, above all, was particularly slow and laborious—according to Pommier and Leleu, it took no less than four years and seven months. See Jean Pommier and Gabrielle Leleu, eds., *Madame Bovary: Nouvelle Version précédée des scénarios inédits* (Paris: J. Corti, 1949), xv.

89. Flaubert, *Correspondance*, 2:411.

90. Flaubert, *Correspondance*, 3:76.

91. Thanks to Melanie Klein and, in the seventies, W. H. Gillespie, psychoanalysis began to reformulate the relationship between perversion and psychosis.

Gustave speaks frequently about his "maladie": he mentions his "horrible anxiety [horrible angoisse]," for example, to Alfred Le Poittevin (*Correspondance*, 1:167), and writes to Louise Colet: "Each attack was a sort of nervous hemorrhage [Chaque attaque était comme une sort d'hémorragie de l'innervation]" (*Correspondance*, 3:270). To Mlle Leroyer de Chantepie he writes: "I often felt that I was going mad. My poor brain was a whirlpool of ideas and images, where my consciousness—my very *self*—was foundering like a ship in a storm [J'ai souvent senti la folie me venir. C'était dans ma pauvre cervelle un tourbillon d'idées et d'images où il me semblait que ma conscience, que mon moi, sombrait comme un vaisseau sous la tempête]" (*Correspondance*, 4:180). See also Charles Carlus, *La Correspondance de Flaubert: Etude et répertoire critique* (Columbus: Ohio State University Press, 1968), 165–72.

92. See Sartre, *L'Idiot*, 1:180ff. and passim, and Marthe Robert, *Roman des origines et origines du roman* (Paris: Gallimard, 1972), 293, 364.

93. Ernest Jones, *The Problem of Hamlet and the Oedipus Complex* (London: Vision Press, 1947).

94. Maurice Nadeau, *Gustave Flaubert, écrivain* (Paris: Denoël, 1969), 126ff.

95. See Sartre, *L'Idiot*, 1:72.

96. Flaubert, *Correspondance*, 5:12.

97. Sartre, *L'Idiot*, 1:83.

98. In Charles's case, it has been seen that masochism and omnipotence are always in league.

99. Flaubert, *Correspondance*, 4:143.

100. Sartre, *L'Idiot*, 1:95–96.

101. Ibid., 1:96.

102. In a letter to Louise Colet dated 12–13 April 1854 (*Correspondance*, 4:58), Flaubert wrote: "I want you male from the waist down; lower down you encumber me, you disturb me, and you are spoiled by the female element [Je te veux homme jusqu'à la hauteur du ventre; en descendant, tu m'encombres et me troubles et t'abîmes avec l'élément femelle]." Nor does the confusion stop there; in the *Correspondance*

(3:166), he compares Louise to Melusine, a woman down to the waist and a serpent below.

103. Flaubert, *Correspondance*, 1:239.

104. As early as 15 January 1853, when he was about to write the second part of *Madame Bovary*, Flaubert told Louise Colet that it had taken him five days to write a single page. In *Après Freud* (Paris: Gallimard, 1968), Jean Baptiste Pontalis points out that Flaubert's desire for precision while writing *Bouvard et Pécuchet*, which, among other things, actually led him to make the journeys undertaken by his two characters, almost suggests a state of hallucination.

105. Flaubert, *Correspondance*, 7:237.

The Barbarous Scythian: An Essay on *King Lear*

1. Gregory Kozintsev, *King Lear, the Space of Tragedy: The Diary of a Film Director*, edited and translated by Mary Mackintosh (London: Heinemann, 1973–77), 18.

2. Peter Brook, *The Empty Space* (London: MacGibbon and Kee, 1968).

3. Søren Kierkegaard, quoted in Kozintsev, *Space*, 23.

4. Kozintsev, *Space*, 49.

5. Among the many themes that run through *King Lear*, I was particularly struck by the one suggested to me by Patrick Mahony: one might contrast the scenes in which the characters use formal, emphatic language with those in which the language is informal. This critical approach might lead to the identification of moments of pure striving for power, for dominion over others, as opposed to moments devoted to the search for authentic truth. In psychoanalytic terms, however, it would lead back to the same point: the ability to endure mental pain and to overcome depression, which are absent from the emphatic language.

The juridical problems raised by *Lear*—those involved in the unilateral promise, the gift, the consent, the solemnity of the process of negotiation—have been considered both in a historical context and from the point of view of general legal theory in Andrea D'Angelo, *Le Promesse unilaterali: Commentario del codice civile* (Milan: Giuffré, 1993).

6. Samuel Leslie Bethell, whose *Shakespeare and the Popular Dramatic Tradition* appeared in 1948 (London: Staples Press), is one of many authors who have interpreted *Lear* as a Christian tragedy.

7. See Andrew Cecil Bradley, *Shakespearean Tragedy* (1904; reprint London: Macmillan, 1922).

8. William Bedell Stanford, *The Ulysses Theme* (Oxford: Blackwell and Matt, 1963), 102.

9. Quotations are from Stanley Wells and Gary Taylor, eds., *The Complete Works of William Shakespeare* (Oxford: Clarendon Press, compact

edition, 1991). Unless otherwise indicated, they are from the Folio text, entitled *The Tragedy of King Lear* (943–74). A *Q* beside the reference indicates that the quotation is taken from the Quarto text, entitled *The History of King Lear* (909–41).

10. J. Wolfgang von Goethe: "Ein alter Mann ist stets ein König Lear."

11. Were the three parts unequal in size and value? If Cordelia's third is "more opulent" and Regan's an "ample third" (1.1.80), then it looks like Lear intended the least attractive third for Goneril. Are these adjectives used rhetorically by the king, or was it his intention to penalize Goneril, the most combative daughter, the one with the strongest personality? The words of Kent and Gloucester at the beginning of the play place Goneril and Regan on the same level.

12. As far as I know, no detailed research has been carried out on the subject, but clinical observation suggests that families who normally exhibit their feelings of love in public (during funeral speeches, for example) tend to harbor narcissism and depression. When all members of a family nucleus accept and share the need to exhibit their feelings, however, it can help alleviate the sense of emptiness and unauthenticity that predominant figures such as parents or grandparents might have unconsciously transmitted to other family members. The exhibition usually evokes echoes of response from subjects who are also depressed. This can give rise to a process of friendship and consensus that, though "defensive," might play a beneficial and to a certain extent reassuring role. The situation in *Lear* is not based on such a premise of consensus.

13. John Holloway, *King Lear* (1961), reprinted in *Shakespeare: King Lear,* edited by Frank Kermode (London: Macmillan, 1992), 193. Among other things, Holloway recalls a significant speech by Cordelia: "O look upon me, sir, / And hold your hand in benediction o'er me. / You must not kneel" (4.6.50–52).

14. See, for example, *Shakespeare's King Lear, Edited with Introduction, Notes, Hints, and Questions,* edited by S. P. B. Mais, assistant master at Sherborne School (London: G. Bell and Sons, 1914), iv.

15. Obviously, Lear does not manipulate only his daughter. For an example of how he tries to manipulate Burgundy, see act 1, scene 1, lines 90–93 ("what in the least will you require").

16. I am indebted to Frank Kermode for this observation.

17. Line 96 does not appear in the Folio edition.

18. This folklore theme is used time and again by Shakespeare according to the cultural codes of his time, but it is also part of his creative imagination. In *An Essay on King Lear* (Cambridge: Cambridge University Press, 1974), S. L. Goldberg quite rightly pointed out that Cordelia is on the defensive at this point.

19. I am referring to the defense mechanism known as "denial" in psychoanalysis.

20. The particular feeling of guilt to which I shall regularly be referring is caused by the violence and predatoriness (whether real or fantasized) of one person toward another. It has its origins in the predatory relationship of the suckling infant with the mother who gives him milk and in the lack of affection that the child may suffer. Once denied and projected, the unconscious destructive fantasies that arise in these circumstances create a sense of danger, menace, and persecution. The greedy or orally denied child fears, above all, being abandoned because of his "greed" or destroying the source that supplied him. Cordelia's *volte-face*, which enables her to deny the fantasy that she has been abandoned and is no longer the favorite child, is one of the mechanisms that act against this fear.

21. Edith Sitwell, among others, had already noted that the roles of Cordelia and the Fool had quite often been played by the same actor. *"King Lear," Atlantic Monthly* 5 (1805): 57–62.

22. Lear will eventually understand just how closely his fragility is associated with his childish omnipotence (apparently even with a final touch of humor) (see 4.5.96–105). He will understand it, but for the wrong reasons.

23. According to Anthony Burgess, Shakespeare must have seen the figure of Saint George for the first time among the frescoes of the Guild Chapel in Stanford before his father had them whitewashed over. See Burgess, *Shakespeare* (London: Cape, 1970), 32–33.

In "Il Barbaro Scita," a psychoanalytic essay on authoritarianism in *King Lear* (*Nuovi Argomenti*, 1978, 59–60), I pointed out that Franco Fornari, in a lecture given at the Milan Institute of Psychoanalysis, November 1976, reexamines the legend of Saint George in order to explain the personalities of those who oppose the violence of authoritarians. He says that there are two types of antiauthoritarian. Those of the first type feel the prevalent need to "deny their own fear of the dragon." They are, then, antipersecutory personalities, whose rebellion against authority assumes a predominantly narcissistic significance. Facing up to the dragon therefore means denying their own fear and persecution anxiety through identification with the persecutor, in order to construct a narcissistic image of themselves as fearless, invulnerable heroes, like Siegfried or fleet-footed Achilles. This is a case of pseudo antiauthoritarian behavior, which finds expression in a paranoid handling of persecution anxiety through identification with the persecutor.

The second type, by contrast, is personified by Saint George and revolves around the figure of the damsel in distress and the feeling of depression that arises if the hero should desert her through fear of the dragon. These personality types are able to accept depression and face the dragon because they feel compelled to save what they love. Furthermore, being able to come to terms with depression, they also succeed in facing the dragon from a realistic standpoint governed by an examination of reality. In other words, the authentic antiauthoritarian personality manages to oppose authority without turning it into a dragon, just as a child manages to oppose his father after having succeeded in divesting him of persecutory projections, which may also be caused by the child's having projected his own destructive impulses onto the parent.

24. Victor Hugo, *William Shakespeare* (Paris, 1864), quoted in Marvin Rosenberg, *The Masks of King Lear* (Berkeley: University of California Press, 1972), 33.

25. Sigmund Freud, *Negation* (*Standard Edition*, 1925), 19:235–39. This remarkable work by Freud has been the subject of essays by various authors from Taine (*Hippolyte*) to Lacan.

26. Perhaps the fact that Cordelia commits suicide in different versions of the Lear story, which Shakespeare probably knew, is not irrelevant to the present interpretation. I realize that this association is methodologically incorrect, but mention it only because in his introduction to the Arden edition of *Lear* (London: Methuen and Co., 1952) Kenneth Muir writes that "in all the sources which are known to have been used by Shakespeare, with only one exception . . . Cordelia commits suicide" (xxxi). Muir makes an interesting comment on Cordelia as a character when he points out that in *The Faerie Queen,* suicide was suggested to Spenser by the need to find a rhyme: "And ouercommen kept in prison long, / Til wearie of that wretched life, her selfe she hong" (quoted in Muir's *Introduction,* xxxi). There is no unconscious motivation, then! With incredible ingenuousness, Muir obstinately refuses to accept the existence of destructive tendencies in the pure figure of Lear's youngest daughter. Idealization can play dirty tricks at times.

27. Enid Welsford, *The Fool: His Social and Literary History* (London: Faber and Faber, 1935).

28. Thus, "to interpret the word 'fool' as a mere insult, a pure and simple pejorative term or, on the contrary, a term of praise, one referring to a sort of 'saint,' is to break up this indissoluble unity." Mikhail Bakhtin, "Tvorcestvo Fransua Rable i narodnaya Kul'tura srednevekov'ya i Renessansa," in *Izdatel'stvo Chudozestvennaya Literatura* (Moscow, 1965). Quoted here from Vanna Gentili's Italian translation, *L'Opera di Rebelais e la cultura popolare* (Turin: Einaudi, 1979), 419–20.

29. In *La Recita della follia* (Turin: Einaudi, 1978), Vanna Gentili writes: "in *King Lear* the figure of the fool . . . is invested with exceptional responsibilities." Here he has lost "much of his shrewd innocence as well

as the ability to represent a reconciliation of opposites . . . and shows a disenchantment that has affinities, on the one hand, with that of the *Vice*, his intriguing progenitor, and, on the other, with that of the cynical philosopher, the malcontent, the acrimonious censor with whom he is about to fuse" (115). Gentili also relates the fool to the "melancholy" figure, noting that "the melancholic is obliged to play the fool," whereas "the fool never plays at being melancholy" (54–55). This insight, which would deserve further commentary, links up with my attempt to demonstrate that from the very beginning Lear's Fool fights all depressive impulses—that is, he seeks a way out of melancholy (understood as depression). In both of these essays I have used the terms "depression" and "melancholy" as synonyms. According to some approaches in psychiatric nosography (themselves discordant), such an equation is incorrect.

30. As it happens, Orwell himself fails to understand the nature of the Fool, whose interventions are described as "a trickle of sanity running through the play." See George Orwell, "Lear, Tolstoy, and the Fool," in *Selected Essays* (Harmondsworth: Penguin, 1957, 101–19). The excerpts from Tolstoy are quoted by Orwell.

31. See Roberta Mullini's interesting essay on the figure of the fool, entitled *Corruttore di parole* (Bologna: Clueb, 1988).

32. Brown interprets Lear's exclamation "And my poor fool is hanged" (5.3.304) literally, although it is often taken to refer to Cordelia.

33. Charles Armitage Brown, *Shakespeare's Autobiographical Poems* (1838), 292, quoted in the *Variorum edition of King Lear*, edited by Horace Howard Furness (New York: Lippincott and Co., 1880), 66.

34. *Variorum*, 67.

35. Robert Hills Goldsmith, *Wise Fools in Shakespeare* (1955; reprint, Liverpool: Liverpool University Press, 1974), 67.

36. *The Diaries of William Charles Macready* (New York, 1912), quoted in *Variorum*, 67–68.

37. Brown, *Poems*, quoted in *Variorum*, 67.

38. Macready, *Diaries*, quoted in *Variorum*, 68.

39. Rosenberg, *Masks*, 107–8.

40. Ibid. While Harley Granville-Barker wanted the Fool to be a "pale-faced boy," and one Japanese Fool stuck so closely to Lear's back that he seemed like a hump, so that the king was forced to turn his head in order to speak to him, Gabriele Baldini considered fools in general "paranoiac," though innocuously so. In his *Manualetto shakespeariano* (Turin: Einaudi, 1964), Baldini writes that in *King Lear* "The Fool's intelligence is not lucid, but it comes in fits and starts and is therefore more intuitive than analytical" (448). For Baldini, the Fool, who is not to be found in any of the numerous sources for *Lear*, is "the most extraordinary character in the whole tragedy" (447). In Ivan Turgenev's short story "A King

Lear of the Steppes" (in *First Love and Other Stories* [Oxford: Oxford University Press, 1982]), the Fool resumes his role as persecuting super-ego: "As soon as I feel sleepy," Martin Petrovic confesses, "somebody inside my head shouts: 'Be careful!'" (203).

41. In his *Projective Identification and Psychotherapeutic Technique* (New York: Aronson, 1982), 11–38, Thomas H. Ogden records the history of this clinical observation and its theorization, beginning with Melanie Klein. Projective identification is connected first of all with a process of the splitting of the self and later with the projection of these separated parts onto others. This unconscious and rather complex process performs both positive functions (it is at the root of empathic communication) and pathological ones: it is used to control, even mold, other people or to offload onto them pain, annoyance, suffering, and so on. Projective identification prompts others to act, to behave according to the dictates that underpin it. An excess of projective identifications prevents the depressed individual from dealing with and *overcoming* his depression. In a surprising essay, *Die Don Juan Gestalt,* dating from 1922, Otto Rank proposes a number of interesting clarifications (see *The Don Juan Legend,* translated and edited by David G. Winter [Princeton: Princeton University Press, 1975], 45–52). First of all, he touches on the idea of projective identification: "The figure of Don Juan, a licentious, unscrupulous knight, fearless before death or the devil, would not have existed if the other side of *Don Giovanni,* i.e., his fear, critical faculties, and conscience had not been projected onto Leporello" (my trans.). In reality Rank accepts these projections of split parts (he speaks of "splits in the personality" of Don Juan) as an aspect of what happens between the author and his characters. In *Some Character-Types Met in Psychoanalytic Work* (1916), *Standard Edition,* 14:309–33, Freud wrote: "Shakespeare often splits a character up into two personages, which, taken separately, are not completely understandable and do not become so until they are brought together once more into a unity" (323). Rank adds that this happens in all the greatest poetical works. He does not, however, describe a factor that Klein was to sense—that this sort of thing occurs in relationships between real people and not merely in the imagination of the poet acting as *deus ex machina.* Rank concludes: "it is not a matter of the (by now banal) psychological conception according to which the poet projects parts of his ego onto his imaginary figures. . . . Rather, it involves quite a special, so to speak secondary, splitting of a character into two figures that together constitute a complete character."

42. Fairbairn has coined the expression "internal saboteur"; see his *Psychoanalytical Studies,* 130. Rosenfeld speaks of "sadistic narcissism." Its cynical, perverse philosophy is not unknown at a clinical level, as Vanna Gentili realized. The saboteur may use tones and language that are kind

and persuasive, even refined (the Fool quotes Aesop!), but is ready to become suddenly violent and threatening whenever he feels under attack.

43. Gregory Bateson, *Steps to an Ecology of Mind* (New York: Chandler, 1972), passim.

44. See Muir's introduction to the Arden edition of *King Lear,* xlvii.

45. Another example of this phallic philosophy is to be found in *Hamlet.* When Laertes hears of Ophelia's death, he says: "and therefore I forbid my tears / but yet . . . let shame say what it will / when these are gone the woman will be out" (4.8.159–62). I have devoted a whole book, *On the Shoulders of Freud: Freud, Lacan, and the Psychoanalysis of Phallic Ideology* (New Brunswick, N.J.: Transaction Publishers, 1991), to phallic philosophy and its antidepressive, maniacal function.

46. See Elias Canetti, "Herrschaft und Paranoia," in *Masse und Macht* (Hamburg: Claassen, 1960), 473–533.

47. *Macbeth* 1.7.54–59.

48. Francis Douce suggests the derivation "Bau Oùv," or artificial phallus. See *Illustrations of Shakespeare,* 2 vols. (1807), 2:319.

49. Note the efficient brevity of the word "jot."

50. *The Anatomy of Melancholy* was completed in 1620 and first published by Burton in 1621 under the pseudonym of Democritus Junior. I have quoted from Robert Burton, *The Anatomy of Melancholy,* edited by Thomas C. Faulkner, Nicholas K. Kiessling, and Rhonda L. Blair, 3 vols. (Oxford: Clarendon Press, 1989), 328.

51. Burton, *Anatomy,* 1:328.

52. Ibid., 1:329.

53. See ibid., 3:203.

54. See ibid., 1:328. From a widely accepted psychoanalytic viewpoint, depression reactivates the first unresolved separations. The production of aggressiveness could reach one of its peaks when the infant is being weaned. Internal objects (such as the Fool) that cause guilt and intense anguish already exist at that stage. Basically, when radicalizing the insights of the writers dear to Burton, many psychoanalysts accept other factors, such as the trauma of birth, but insist that adult depression cannot be understood without an awareness of primary depression.

55. It would be more correct at this point to speak of a preambivalent position, where love and hate are not perceived as being in conflict but rather coexist as split parts. In this situation the parts that hate are projected outward. (Lear's projections will be discussed below.) "True" ambivalence sets in with a growing awareness that feelings of love and hatred toward the same person are in conflict with each other. It will be shown that Lear is unable to reach this stage in a complete and stable sense.

With introjection (or, rather, reintrojection), the self of the melancholy person *splits* into the sadistic part that has suffered traumatic abandonment (in this case, the Fool) and the part that is attacked: the Lear–barbarous Scythian part has devoured Cordelia and is now tortured instead of her. This is the central discovery in Freud's *Mourning and Melancholy*. Psychoanalytic theory has distanced itself from Abraham and Freud's first formulation: the cannibalistic mechanism of introjection is certainly there to combat the traumatizing loss, but identification with the object involves both the attacked and the attacking part. In the final analysis, the latter is a conglomerate: the Fool comprises Cordelia as well as the childish parts of Lear. This develops the autarchic, phallic, and antidepressive "philosophies" found in the pronouncements of the king's jester.

56. Freud called this "the compulsion to repeat."

57. The theme of the "emotional tempest" caused by depression ("This tempest in my mind" [2.6.188]), which Shakespeare left unresolved in this tragedy, would be taken up again and given a quite different solution in a late play entitled (probably not by mere coincidence) *The Tempest*.

58. Hecate appears at midnight, the Fool leaves at midday, just as Lear is about to meet Cordelia who, following the storm of depression, is once more a good fairy:

Lear: We'll go to supper in the morning.
Fool: And I'll go to bed at noon. (3.6.42–43)

Depression is experienced by the narcissistic-sadistic part (the Fool) not as an opportunity to change but as a mortal threat: to accept the need of another is to end one's narcissistic isolation.

In *The Theme of the Three Caskets, Standard Edition,* 12:299, Freud places Artemis-Hecate among the great mother divinities of the oriental peoples. Such deities are both life-giving and life-destroying, goddesses at once of life and fertility and of death.

59. Deprivation and hunger are very closely connected in both myths and fairy tales: *Hansel and Gretel, Little Red Riding Hood,* and *Tom Thumb* are well-known examples of the way being abandoned by a mother causes a hungry rage that is then projected onto the witch, the wolf, and the ogre. We should not be misled by the fact that this hunger (caused less by biological appetite than by the anxiety occasioned by desertion and the lack of good enough mothering, signs of unresolvable future voids: the infant sucks its finger even when it is sated with milk) is often attributed to a paternal substitute (the ogre in *Tom Thumb,* the wolf in *Little Red Riding Hood*). Fornari calls this phenomenon primary "paranoia." The witch, the ogre, and the wolf arise from the inability to

continue keeping the other person inside as a kindly presence, as a breast that goes on offering warmth and milk. When the good, caring mother can be recovered through recollection (which is not always possible), the tragedy of the melancholic begins to dissolve.

60. Following the work of the psychoanalyst John Bowlby, many researchers, especially in the United States, have studied the patterns according to which infants become attached to their mothers. Mary Main's "Security in Infancy, Childhood, and Adulthood," in Inge Bretherton and Edward Waters, *Growing Points of Attachment Theory and Research* (Monograph Society for Research in Child Development, no. 209, vol. 50:66–104), identifies a category of "reverse attachment," where a son or daughter tends to behave like a parent toward his/her mother or father. This is the pattern I have been outlining of Lear's relationship with his three daughters.

61. I am referring to the forbidden apple (the breast) and the journey out of the maternal womb: "And the eyes of them both were opened" (*Genesis* 3:7)—i.e., they saw the light of day, were born.

62. This phenomenon is well known to all psychoanalysts who have dealt with deep levels of depression. It is not clear to me why it occurs; I find Meltzer's hypothesis in *The Psychoanalytic Process* (London: Heinemann, 1967) unconvincing.

63. See the essay on Charbovari.

64. The *Oxford English Dictionary* defines "ass" as "vulgar and dialect spelling and pronunciation of arse." As for the rarer meaning, the *Random House Dictionary* offers, "a woman considered an object of coitus," a woman therefore seen as "a vagina," a partial, narcissistic object. "Ass" derives from the common Teutonic noun "harse." In the glossary of *Shakespeare's Bawdy* (1947; reprint, London: Routledge and Kegan Paul, 1961), Eric Partridge confirms Shakespeare's use of "ass" as synonym for "arse." However, Partridge does not seem to support his assertion with valid arguments, and the *Oxford English Dictionary* does not bear him out. In a personal letter, Anthony Burgess suggested that I should tread carefully on this matter and doubted that this meaning was already current in Shakespeare's day. Burgess was probably right and Partridge wrong. However, I believe my hypothesis can still be supported on the following grounds: the somewhat dated examples given in the *Oxford English Dictionary*, although almost always correct, are not totally reliable. Giuseppe Sertoli, for example, has reminded me that about a century after *Lear* was written, in chapter 32 of *Tristram Shandy*, Laurence Sterne makes an entire dialogue between Tristram's father and Uncle Toby turn on the double meaning of the word "ass." This is ignored by the *Oxford English Dictionary*. There are other, more cogent arguments: Shakespeare associates "ass" and "bottom" in *A Midsummer*

Night's Dream, where the weaver Bottom wears an ass's head. If the "ass-arse" association had not entered everyday usage, it certainly existed in the poet's preconscious mind.

As for the connection between "woman" and "ass" (in the sense of the Latin *asinum*), in Trieste "mula" (mule) is used to mean "girl," and in a number of patrocentric cultures, it is the task of the woman to carry heavy loads.

65. . . . if thus thou wilt appear, / Freedom lives hence" (1.1.180). Kent appears to be drastically embracing the thesis of Etienne de La Boétie, who, having studied and reworked the great myths of the classical world, rejected any condemnation inflicted by a monarch as in all cases tyrannical.

66. Paul Alfred Jorgensen, *Lear's Self-Discovery* (Berkeley: University of California Press, 1967), 76–77, 84.

67. The Italian actor Carlo Cataneo, who played Kent in many performances of Strehler's production, admitted to me that he had come to hate Kent's "nobility" profoundly.

68. There are three versions of these lines: Q1, Q2, and F. See Frank Kermode, *Disintegration Once More* (Proceedings of the British Academy, 1994, 84, 93–111), which shows just how complicated the question is. In the Folio text, the whole sentence runs: "Such smiling rogues as these, / Like rats, oft bite the holy cords a-twain, / Which are too intrince t'unloose, smooth every passion / That in the natures of their lords rebel / Being oil to fire, snow to the colder moods / Renege, affirm, and turn their halcyon beaks / With every gale and vary of their masters / Knowing naught—like dogs—but following" (2.2.73–80). Kent's tirade continues in an excited, manic crescendo (2.2.81–84) that prompts Cornwall to say, "What, art you mad, old fellow?"

69. "Smoothes" is another incredibly ambiguous word. Does it mean "regulates," "calms down," or perhaps "facilitates"?

70. It has always been correctly assumed that in this passage ("O, how this mother swells up toward my heart! / *Hysterica passio* down, thou climbing sorrow / Thy element's below" [2.2.231–33]), "mother" means "uterus." The reference to hysteria makes it a certainty. Here, Lear refers to a phenomenon calls *bolus hystericus*, probably because he feels a tightness in his throat. From the time of Hippocrates right through to the seventeenth century, it was believed that the uterus could travel as far as the throat and cause an obstruction to breathing. Thomas Willis then decided to use a scalpel to check whether the uterus really did move in such a way. "Uterus" is to "mother" as a part is to the whole, it is a synecdoche—perhaps an unconscious one in this case. The expression is certainly thought-provoking. Why does Lear identify with a woman?

Because of an identification with the aggressor? And why does he diagnose himself as a hysteric?

71. Kent had earlier claimed to be the king's twin in poverty (1.4.19–20).

72. Shakespeare also plays on the double meaning of "rotten" in the graveyard scene in *Hamlet:*

Hamlet: How long will a man lie i' the earth ere he rot?
First Clown: I' faith, if a' be not rotten before a' die. . . . (5.1.159–60)

See also *Pericles* 4.2.7–9.

73. In that masterpiece of ambivalence "Filial Feelings of a Matricide" (*Le Figaro,* 1 February 1907), Marcel Proust puts his finger on Kent's ambiguity when quoting his words to Edgar, who "wants to revive the unconscious king" (Lear has not fainted, as Proust says, but is dead):

Vex not his ghost. O let him pass. He hates him
That would upon the rack of this tough world
Stretch him out longer. (5.3.289–91)

74. Among the works I have consulted are Rosalie L. Colie, "Reason and Need: *King Lear* and the 'Crisis' of the Aristocracy" (a comment on Lawrence Stone's study), in *Some Faces of King Lear: Essays in Prismatic Criticism,* edited by R. L. Colie and F. T. Flahiff (Toronto: University of Toronto Press, 1974), 185–220, and *Shakespeare's Tragic Heroes* by Lily Bess Campbell (Cambridge: Cambridge University Press, 1930). For an interesting overview of the philosophical problem of *nosce te ipsum,* see also the chapter entitled "Some Renaissance Contexts" in Jorgensen, *Self-Discovery,* and Paul N. Siegel, *Shakespeare in His Time and Ours* (London: University of Notre Dame Press, 1968).

75. *Hamlet* 3.2.22.

76. Frederich James Furnivall, *The Babees Book* (London: Trübner, 1868), 330.

77. See Philippe Ariès, *L'Enfant et la vie familiale sous l'Ancien Régime* (Paris: Editions du Seuil, 1973). *Italian translation: Padri e figli nell'Europa medievale moderna* (Bari: Laterza, 1968).

78. A. Varet, *De l'éducation chrétienne des enfants* (1666), quoted in Ariès, *Padri e figli,* 436–37.

79. Alessandro Serpieri, "The Breakdown of Medieval Hierarchy" in *Shakespearian Tragedy,* edited by John Drakakis (London: Longman, 1992), 84–95. On the same subject, see Jorgensen, *Self-Discovery,* 7.

80. From the *Mémoires de Louis XIV pour l'instruction du Dauphin* (1661).

81. In the sense explored by Bateson in *Steps to an Ecology.*

82. I am grateful to Pier Luigi Sommaruga for this suggestion.

83. In *Shakespeare and the Critics* (Cambridge: Cambridge University Press, 1972), 144–205, A. L. French makes a magisterial analysis of the "mistakes" committed by Goneril and Regan before the storm. Much of his interpretation agrees with mine. He shows that Lear is obviously not sent away by his daughters but leaves of his own accord. In act 3, scene 6, lines 15–16, the father is encouraged by the Fool in his fantasies "To have a thousand with red, burning spits / Come hissing in upon 'em!"

84. See the discussion of Kent above.

85. See Alice Miller in *Das Drama des begabten Kindes und die Suche nach dem wahren Selbst* (Frankfurt: Suhrkamp, 1979). Even though some of the theoretical and clinical options expressed by Miller are debatable, she must be credited with having clearly emphasized this problem.

86. On this subject, Franco Fornari has spoken of equal codes that are in competition: in order to be fulfilled, the code of the child's demand must meet the code of parental readiness to supply. See Fornari's *Il Codice vivente* (Turin: Boringhieri, 1981).

87. Gloucester reminds Lear of Cornwall's "fiery quality" (2.4.94), but Lear will not listen.

88. Suffice it to recall the violence of the orders Lear gives to Kent (3.2.7; 4.6.188, etc.).

89. See Bradley, *Shakespearean Tragedy*, 00.

90. G. Melchiori perceives an intersecting of the "historical" and the "eternal" in *Lear*. See his introduction to *Teatro completo di William Shakespeare* 4 (Milan: Mondadori, 1976).

91. For a discussion of David Pareus, see Giuseppe Giarizzo, "Il pensiero inglese nell'età degli Stuard e della Rivoluzione," in *L'Età moderna*, vol. 4, *Storia delle Idee politiche, economiche e sociali*, Luigi Firpo, General Editor, 7 vols. (Turin: UTET, 1970), 1:181–83.

92. These lines are omitted from Q1.

93. These lines are omitted from F.

94. Gloucester calls Edmond a "whoreson" (1.1.23). In the context, the term could sound to Edmond more like an insult to his mother than an affectionate term for him. Nor is it by chance that Edmond ironically refers to the mother of the legitimate children as "honest madam" (1.2.9).

95. Although whole books have been written on the concept of "Nature" in Shakespeare (e.g., John Danby, *Shakespeare's Doctrine of Nature* [London: Faber and Faber, 1949]), in Freudian terms "nature" is the symbol of the mother (Mother Earth).

96. In an authoritarian relationship the child's real interests are secondary to the parent's need to obtain responses that will gratify his narcissism. This need leads him to expect and, at times, indirectly to beg for

strength and esteem in a magical and therefore ephemeral manner. The dependent subject is thus transformed by projective identification into a phantasmal source of supply: the parent becomes the child, and the child becomes the parent. This is what happens in the case of Lear and his daughters.

97. York's words in *Richard II*.

Index

Roberto Speziale-Bagliacca, Professor of Psychotherapy in the Medical Faculty of the University of Genoa and training analyst of the Italian and the International Psychoanalytic Association, has worked on the mind-body relationship in various cultures and on the theoretical and clinical aspects of psychoanalysis in relation to their ideological content and their place in the history of ideas. His works have been translated into many languages; among them, in English, is *On the Shoulders of Freud: Lacan and the Psychoanalysis of Phallic Ideology* (1991). For a number of years he has contributed articles to *Nuovi Argomenti*, the journal in which Alberto Moravia published the first versions of the two essays contained in this volume. His latest book, *Colpa* (Guilt), has recently appeared in Italian.

Library of Congress Cataloging-in-Publication Data

Speziale-Bagliacca, Roberto.
[Crescere corvi. English]
The king and the adulteress : a psychoanalytic and literary reinterpretation of
Madame Bovary and King Lear / Roberto Speziale-Bagliacca ; foreword by
Frank Kermode ; translated by Aina Pavolini Taylor ; edited by Colin Rice.
p.   cm.
"A revised edition of Crescere corvi : psicoanalisi di Madame Bovary e Re
Lear."
Includes index.
ISBN 0-8223-2075-4 (alk. paper). — ISBN 0-8223-2089-4 (pbk. : alk. paper)
1. Flaubert, Gustave, 1821–1880. Madame Bovary.   2. Shakespeare,
William, 1564–1616. King Lear.   3. Psychoanalysis and literature.   I. Title.
PQ2246.M3S66   1998
843'.8—dc21   97-17772